LOVE LESSONS

Also by George Davis

Coming Home: A Novel
Love, Black Love
Black Life in Corporate America
Soul Vibrations

LOVE LESSONS

African Americans and Sex, Romance, and Marriage in the Nineties

GEORGE DAVIS

William Morrow and Company, Inc. New York

It is the policy of William Morrow and Company, Inc., and its imprints and affiliates, recognizing the importance of preserving what has been written, to print the books we publish on acid-free paper, and we exert our best efforts to that end.

Library of Congress Cataloging-in-Publication Data

Davis, George, 1939–
    Love lessons : African Americans and sex, romance, and marriage in the nineties / George Davis.
        p.   cm.
    ISBN 0-688-14864-6
    1. Afro-Americans—Social life and customs.   2. Afro-Americans—Psychology.   3. Love.   I. Title.
    E185.86.D3855   1998

                                                    97-28865
                                                    CIP

Printed in the United States of America

First Edition

2   3   4   5   6   7   8   9   10

BOOK DESIGN BY LEAH S. CARLSON

www.williammorrow.com

For the lover in each of us

ACKNOWLEDGMENTS

I would like to thank the hundreds of people who consented to be interviewed for this book, and especially those whose stories were selected to be included. I would also like to acknowledge with special gratitude Audrey Coleman, Al Dyer, and Tobe Onugha, who did some of the interviewing.

CONTENTS

LOVE LESSONS

INTRODUCTION

*I*n a familiar phrase we often say that *the more things change, the more they remain the same.* But it's also true that *the more things change, the more they differ from the way they used to be.* Both phrases seem to be true of love.

Twenty years ago I wrote *Love, Black Love,* a book about love, based on interviews. In 1996 I started interviewing again, asking the same questions: What is love? How long does it last? Is it light enough to play with? Is it serious enough to drive you crazy? Is it fun? Is it useful? If it fails the first time, do you want it to come again? Can you love, really love, two people at once? Or three? Does money make the heart grow fonder?

The questions are the same, but at times the answers are very different. This book is about some of those differences, and about the lessons about love that our changing times have taught us.

A dictionary that I used in the early seventies I still use today, so of course it gives the same definition of the word *love:* "1. an intense affectionate concern for another person; 2. an intense sexual desire for another person."

Back in the 1970s I wanted to create a book about what happened when people attempted to express that intense affectionate concern or that intense sexual desire. This book is about what happens now when we try. The love stories here, like those in the former book, have been fictionalized to guarantee the anonymity of those who agreed to speak candidly on so intimate a subject.

The things that people had to say about love back then were

sometimes funny, sometimes touching. Now they are less of either. They are more searching, more cautious, more thoughtful. People seem to have a deeper interest in what happens to the rest of their lives as a result of love. Finding love isn't now as much a matter of fools rushing in where wise men fear to go, as the old familiar song says.

The new theme song seems to be that you've got to be ba-a-ad. You've got to be hard. You've got to be tough. You've got to be self-involved, as Deseree sings in her 1996 hit.

"In the 1990s love has become a rarity," said a young woman in Washington whose tender love story is told here in "Being There for Love." She said, "You don't even hear about it much anymore, much less witness love that is selfless, where one person positively and joyfully cares about the other person's well-being and happiness."

A young woman in New York who has been very successful as a financial adviser to rich and famous clients said that love may be the same, but that it "is tied to a lot of other things for me. Love is a deal for me, and if the man doesn't bring enough to the table, then there's no deal," she said in a story called "A Nineties Kinda Love."

"I'm still like I was twenty years ago," said a man I interviewed for the first book and then interviewed again for this one. "I'm still afraid of love, although I wouldn't use the word *afraid* now." In a story then called "A Love Affair," and a story now called "The More Love Changes," he reveals that he has had a happy love life by accepting the fact that he doesn't like love when it gets too intense.

A seventeen-year-old who feels he has spent his childhood dodging real bullets on the mean streets of Baltimore said: "Nobody talks about love anymore. It's not about that. It's about survival. It's about the car you drive." He says that in his world "women have been taught that it's all about economics."

Back in the 1970s my friend Mervyn Taylor said love among black people "is love in a narrow space. For us," he said, "love is not a matter of pledging troth beneath the sky and walking off into the sunset to live happily ever after.

"It may involve a brief meeting in a darkened room somewhere, or coming down a stairs and parting, each to go his or her own way. Often it's a matter of making do, of stealing sweetness from the night, with no illusions about permanence."

Mervyn is a poet, and so this was his rather lyrical way of saying that there were a lot of different pressures and influences in black life that gave love some interestingly different flavors back then.

An even more confusing assortment of factors are caught up in it now. We know from the blues tradition that black love often had to bear the weight of the world. All the wounds of life—unemployment, underemployment, homelessness, racial indignities, drug or alcohol addiction—had to be healed by the love relationship. This is what Marvin Gaye sings about in "Sexual Healing."

But in the nineties so many seem to have moved beyond that tradition to the extent that they now believe that neither sex nor love can heal most of life's wounds.

"What is love in the nineties? I guess I should know since I'm married and should be in love," said a corporate executive in Connecticut. "Love is being satisfied with things that your emotions tell you that you don't really like, but you put up with them because you convince yourself that they are a normal part of life."

He and his wife own a big beautiful house. When asked why he didn't sell the house, get a divorce, and go searching to be healed by love, he said: "What good would that do? Go where? I don't have anyone else that I want to spend my life with," he said in a story called "Love in a Dream House."

Often, back in the 1970s, both sex and love did become a matter of stealing sweetness from the night. And now so many of us and our children are serving time for the sweetness we stole from so many of those nights back in a decade when the rituals, traditions, and customs of church, family, and community began to fade in the face of the Sexual Revolution, the Black Revolution, the Women's Movement, and the Revolution of Rising Expectations.

We did a lot of crazy things in the name of love. One of the results of the love we felt and the things we did back then was that now many of our children seem to be afraid of marriage because of our high divorce rate.

"I was completely against marriage. There are a lot of people my age who don't believe in marriage because of what we saw our parents go through," said one young woman, in "Love's Gonna Get Ya." She said: "At a very young age I was caught in the middle of a knock-down, drag-out, police-calling, ugly-for-years divorce."

In twenty years not only did love change but I changed. The old book feels very different from the new one because back in the 1970s, I remember that I was quite frantically searching for some emotional or spiritual truths that would make love work well in my life. And I was disturbed and involved in a rampaging search to try to find out what love really was after I concluded that it was not what I wanted it to be.

Now I am more willing to accept it for what it is. I am more an observer and reporter on other people's search than a searcher myself. I am not looking to verify or refute some tentative feelings of my own. I am more in search of tribal truths, even as the African-American tribe is being mixed into the multiculture that America is fast becoming.

*　　*　　*

Love, Black Love provided me with some good training for the writing of this book. Back then, for example, I did all the interviewing; but this time I wanted to see what different kinds of interviewees would say to different kinds of interviewers.

Some of the interviews for this book were done by Audrey Coleman, a woman of thirty-five, born and reared in Little Rock, Arkansas. I knew her when she was six years old. She is a reaper of some of what our generation sowed back in the days of *Love, Black Love*.

I wanted her to interview two men her age who were in love and two men who were not. She said the two men who were not would be easy to find. I said, "Dag, Audrey! I hope you can find the other two."

"I'm having a really hard time."

"In the whole city of Little Rock? There are more than a hundred fifty thousand people, more than forty thousand black folk."

"Actually, it's been a lot of fun just talking to these guys. Most of the men I know are married, and most of the men don't really love their wives. They got married for reasons other than love—looks, sex.

"A lot of these guys I know were in college and probably part of the woodwork. They graduated from school, went to med school, law school, and began experiencing popularity they had never experienced before. They had access to a lot of women, which they didn't have before.

"They marry women who are more excited about what they are than who they are," Audrey said.

Audrey and I didn't find that black love in the 1990s was love in a "narrow space." The doors had been thrown open. Idealists are still finding themselves in love with materialists. Serious seekers still fall in love with players; the deep and intense get hooked on the fly and superficially; homebodies get captured by lovers of the street life, and vice versa.

But the conditions have changed so much. At one end, black life is more deeply affected by homelessness and poverty, as in the story "The 'We' That Love Creates," or, at the other end, by affluence, as in a number of these stories.

On the other hand, hundreds of thousands of black people have, sometimes smoothly and sometimes not, worked their way into the major economic and political institutions of the nation.

An accountant, an attorney, a corporate vice president, a financial adviser, thinks differently about love than someone who has nothing much else to think about, as was true with many of the interviewees in *Love, Black Love*. What people learn in their professions leaks over into the way they love and accept love.

In the 1970s we were closer to the period "when love was all we had." Back in the 1970s I noted that "we black Americans (all exceptions admitted), with our fragile egos and large expectations, love love. We curse and cut each other more often, but we own more 'I love you, shoo-be-do' phonograph records than any other people of twice our number on this planet." It is hard to tell if this is true anymore.

We used to sit up all night listening to "loving you is easier than breathing." Some of us grew up in houses where the messages were repeated from get-up in the morning to lie-down at night— "Stay, darling, stay in my corner"; "Hypnotized"; "Just one look, that's all it took"; "Love is all I need to get by."

Now so many of us have to clear our heads and go to bed early to be ready to get out to a professional job in the morning, or to get up to begin the search for a way to sustain ourselves without a job.

"In the 1990s you don't have as much time for love. You spend all your time focused on the behavior you need to get the things that you either need or think you need to survive," said a financial planner whose story appears here as "Love in Greener Grass." "You don't have the time or the interest in concentrating on what you need to do to make another person happy."

Back then we walked the streets with transistors plugged into our ears with somebody crooning reassuringly, "Love is the answer," or, "Love lifted me this morning."

Singers are still doing love songs. There was this one in 1996 by a preteenage songstress named Monica: "Baby that's just why I love you so much. Baby that's just why I can't get enough."

In the 1990s Barry White still crooned that you got to keep looking for love, and that love will always be the icon for everyone's search, all over the world.

Meanwhile, many of the people from all over the world have come to America. Most did not come looking for love, but many will have to try to find it in the course of finding an American life.

The newcomers add a tempting new element to the searches of those who were born here. In the story "What If Love . . . ?" a young woman from West Africa says she believes that "The songs on the radio, that's what's got this culture messed up. True love is not like you hear it all the time on the radio."

She speculates a lot on what life would be like if love was as it was for her grandparents in a small village in Ghana, where a man didn't just marry a woman, he married into her matrifocal, extended family, after he had been screened for suitability by the entire family.

In the 1990s people still walk the streets with radios, but not always with ear plugs. Sometimes the guys have their boom boxes turned up as loud as they will go. They want everyone to dig Kurtis Blow's rap that you've got to be ready to pack your bags, kiss your woman, say good-bye simply because there might not be room in your life for a woman, especially, as Full force sings: "not the kind that will hover."

They are reacting to, or causing the reactions of, anger and disenchantment of the black women expressed in *Waiting to Exhale:* "I'm gonna pack my cares away. Got no cause to look back. I'm looking for a better day."

The way it is for African Americans in the nineties is not all that different than it is for Americans in general. It seems that so often black people experience nothing more than extremely complicated versions of what all Americans are experiencing here at the end of the millennium.

A white housewife who lives outside Muncie, Indiana, said that her suburban daughter walks around their suburban split-level home singing the Deseree song about being ba-a-ad, hard, and tough. Both of her sons love rap music.

Some resist the recent anger, which is why oldie-but-goodie radio stations flourish by playing the old "I love you, shoo-be-do" songs from the past.

And millions of copies of various books of inspiration sell to African-American book buyers. Most of the inspiration is for the kind of spiritually-oriented search for love and connectedness that is expressed here in stories like "Being Loved" and "Love Don't Need No Reasons."

Thousands of young men came back from the Million Man March and made loving commitments to their wives, estranged wives, girlfriends, and mothers of their babies. Many young women, especially those in college, speak of love in the context of family.

"When I think of love in the 1990s, I always think of family. There are now so many black family reunions in all parts of the country. The love you share with your family is shared when your husband becomes a part of your family and you become a part of his," said a young woman who was a member of a group of college students I interviewed in Newark, New Jersey.

Despite the persistence of racism, racially mixed couples seemed to be more plentiful than they were in the 1970s, and there seemed to be a difference between the ones I knew then and the ones I know now. Back then the couples were more often rebels against their individual black or white communities. Now the communities themselves have dissolved and the rebellion, when necessary, seems to be against those who'd like to hold on to the fragments of racial solidarity by claiming all those of the same race as "our women" or "our men" and all those of a different race as "their women" and "their men."

The children of the racially mixed couples of the 1970s are old enough now to be looking for love. In the story "Love in a Swirl of Colors," a man whose father was black and mother was Italian said one of his biggest love problems was determining who "our women" and "our men" really were: "Black women would talk to me in a certain way because I'm not totally black, whatever that means, and white women would talk to me in a certain way because I'm not totally white, whatever that means.

"I wasn't rejected. I found it easy to date either race of women. The problem was that I didn't feel included with either. Women from each race talked to me as if I was a member of the other race."

What odd and powerful collections of cultural and racial factors create the awareness of what it does or does not mean to be a black woman or a black man; and what a powerful collection of expectations and dreams determines what each of us chooses and/or avoids in sex, lifestyle, and love, usually for reasons that have little to do with race and more to do with how the individual human spirit responds to intimacy in the rapidly changing world of the 1990s.

BEING THERE FOR Love

"One reason I didn't want to deal with Jennifer at first is that she reminded me of my mother, and you know all that stuff about a man looking for a woman who can mother him—I didn't even want that in it, especially since my mother had such a strong influence on my life," Albert said.

Albert and I were riding in his delivery van south on Interstate 395, leaving Washington, D.C., heading for the Capital Beltway. He was speeding, so he kept looking in the rearview, watching out for "the man." "The man" was his name for cops.

"So you would just automatically not want to love any woman who in any way reminded you of your mother?" I asked. It was a winter day but very sunny, and with the windows of the van closed the thing that was most indicative of winter was the branches of trees, which were either bare or clustered with brown leaves. The sky was clear and blue.

"Yeah, I certainly didn't want any woman to have the power over me that my mother had. I wouldn't want to have that in my mind while I was dealing with her." He was one of those dark Nubian blacks. He looked like a fat Michael Jordan.

Remembering Jennifer, I asked him if she looked like his mother. He said no. Jennifer was light-skinned. His mother was a dark woman. Jennifer was small. His mother, when she was alive, was a big woman, he said.

"You loved her?"

"I was very close to my mother before she died," he said.

15

Albert is a huge man with a belly that is big probably as much from eating cornbread and collard greens as from drinking beer.

"You're very close to Jennifer?"

"Yeah, Jennifer's all right," he said in a matter-of-fact way. "She's like my mother, though. She thinks like my mother, and you know what spooked me at first?"

"What?"

"She and mother have the same birth date."

"Do you believe in signs?"

"Not really."

"When is her birth date?"

"They're both Capricorns—January 15."

"Martin Luther King's birthdate."

"Yeah! Yeah! Yeah! I know." He pulled his baseball cap farther around to the side, as if to say, I can't believe that this happened to me. "My brothers, they both married women who look like my mother, but one of the reasons I joined the service was to get away from my mother, and so I dated wild women, all kinds of women—German women, New York women, California women, Vietnamese women—I took the grand tour." He had a big laugh.

"And came back home."

"Yup! I can't believe it." He scratched his cap as if it were his head. We were scooting along on his delivery route. He worked for a stationery supplier in Washington that had a lot of customers out in northern Virginia. "Maybe it's just that she's a Southern woman. Maybe that's it."

"Could be. Could be."

Jennifer worked in a Giant Supermarket in D.C. I had interviewed Jennifer two days earlier. She had told me to catch Albert and find out what he would say.

She was petite, with a short reddish hairdo cut into bangs. She was one of those feisty yella girls from down around Culpeper, Virginia.

She had a gentle laugh that did not stop when she spoke. She could laugh and speak at the same time. Her words laughed. "Tell Albert not to lie," she said. We were eating lunch in Arby's with a bunch of the other women who worked in Giant. They all wore the red smocks with the white name tags. Above their names was the store's motto: "Giant cares for you."

We had joked for a while about the relationship between love and groceries. They all agreed that with a lot of men they knew out of work, and a lot of single mothers raising children, there was a strong relationship between love and groceries.

"It's important for a man to be able to bring home the groceries," Jennifer said.

"Would that make the big difference?" I asked, and the joking responses ranged from "Hell, yeah" to "Not at all." Jennifer said it made a difference, but that was not all there was to it. "Catch Albert, see what he says love is," she said.

"You don't mind?" I asked her.

"No. He might put a little more to it, but basically it will be as it is. It will be as he says it is."

I said to Albert as he drove, "She seems like a nice lady." He kept looking in the rearview mirror, seeming to enjoy outwitting "the man.' " He said he had gotten three speeding tickets in the last year, and a cop had taken away his illegal radar detector.

"Jennifer? Jennifer? What did she tell you?" he said, seeming not to want to let on that he was as curious as he was.

"She said that love for her meant being there."

He stopped looking in his rearview mirror and took a good look at me. "Is that what she said?"

I recalled that Jennifer had said: "Being there. That's love??" The other women were sitting there listening to her, making sure she didn't say anything too wrong. "That's caring," she said. "Being there." She stopped talking to laugh this time, and the laugh seemed to rock something inside her, like a mother rocks a cradle.

"I think that love is not just being there," I said in a tone that would provoke her to talk more. She was perky. I knew she was not going to let me just contradict her. "It's not just caring in a passive way. It is about doing something to help someone. Love is a verb too, not just a noun. It's not always about letting it be as it is, as you say."

"Caring is about doing something. Caring is about speaking your mind even in disagreement, just to make some points here. Yeah, I sure agree with that. But often times you know that you can't do anything because of the consequences. You can't."

"Okay, but that's rough, to see someone you love making mistakes, and you know that when it doesn't turn out right, you're going to have to be there. You can go through that without saying anything?"

"That's one of life's fates. Yeah. We're at the finish. We know how to go in and come out, and can tell them how to—not that you can do it for them, but they've got to go through it, and you've still got to stand there and wait for them when they come out."

"Whew! Okay. That's tough."

She laughed again with the laugh that seemed to rock something inside her, but it wasn't like rocking a baby. It was like rocking something very old. "One of the mazes of life," she said, almost under her breath.

"What is love?"

"When you're first in love you see the world in a different

light. Everything is just beautiful to you, when you're first in love.'' She spoke as if she were reciting the lyrics to a song.

"Yeah, what causes that?''

"The other person. The chemistry between you. You're happy because of the way you are and the way the other person is.''

"And after that what is love?''

"Being there.''

"Being there.''

"Being there.''

"And caring?''

"And caring. I care. I care what happens to him. I want good things to happen to him because he has a good heart.''

"Albert?''

"Yeah.''

In the delivery van that December morning I asked Albert: "You've been married nine years?''

"And three kids,'' he said. "Her mother keeps the kids. That's why we live in D.C. mainly. There's a whole extended family in D.C. My wife has five sisters and one brother in D.C. The mother runs something like a day-care center for all of us. She's a sweet woman. We all call her Mom—her three sons-in-law and daughter-in-law.''

"Is Jennifer like her mother?''

"No, she's more like her father. He sits around as if he knows something that nobody else knows.''

"Like Jennifer?''

"Like Jennifer!'' He screamed because he was glad I knew what he was talking about.

"Like your mother used to?''

"I guess.''

"She told me to ask you what love is.''

He was in the middle of explaining when we made his first delivery, at a big office complex out on Route 7 past Tysons Corner. When we got back inside the van he said: "I don't know. I don't think about it in terms of love. I think about it in terms of being a fool or messing up. In that way you can still be a man, still keep on looking, because there are some nice ladies out here to look at and just because you're married you don't stop—oh, 'I'm in love so I don't want to be with another lady,' but I'm not a fool. I'm not going to mess up because when you mess up you don't only mess yourself up."

"So love is not messing up?"

"Not just that, but generally."

"What do you mean by mess up?"

"Mess up with another woman. Yeah, my old lady's slick. If I messed with another woman, she would know."

I remember what Jennifer had said when I asked her how she would know. She said she just would. I told her that that was no answer. "How?"

"You ask a woman," she had said. "You just know."

"Clues?"

"You don't look for clues. You don't sit around and look for clues. You just know."

"But suppose you don't know?"

"Then it doesn't matter. More power to everybody."

"But you just say that because you know he's not messing up."

"That was my point here," she had said.

We had made another delivery and stopped to get a McDonald's bacon, egg, and cheese biscuit. "Jennifer's slick," he said as he enjoyed his biscuit. "She keeps telling me that she knows that I would never do anything, so that trust that she puts in me, which is the reason she puts the trust in me in the first place, means that I don't want to betray that trust.

"She keeps making love to this ideal man that she keeps telling me that I am and so that makes me want to be that man. She's slick. She told you about the mazes?"

"Yeah."

"I know she told you about the mazes. She had to tell you about the mazes. That's from her father. He sits around talking about something being in the maze. 'You can't rush 'em. You can't rush at 'em. You just have to wait.' " He imitated his father-in-law's voice. He had a big, satisfying laugh.

"It works."

"Yeah, it works for them."

"You're happy."

"Not all the time."

"You're happy with her."

"Yeah, I mean, what can you do? I have a very hot temper and she has a lot of patience. I don't know. I get upset easily about a lot of stuff. I come home sometimes yelling and raising hell about the rat race, and I just need somebody to unload on. When I'm going through it, I curse everybody and anybody—'Get the fuck out of here.' But then I know she likes the rewarding that I do because she was there for me.

"I get it out of my system and then I become very appreciative of her, you know, because I trusted that she knew how to handle this madness. And that's what made me open up and she likes that. After I've been an asshole, I can open up because I have to tell her why I was such an asshole.

"And I know that makes her feel needed and then there is the rewarding. Very often our best times are tied up in the rewarding, and so we wouldn't have those good times if I wasn't an asshole in the first place. So it all works out."

"That's love," I said.

He smiled because he knew I had him.

The next time I called Jennifer at home her youngest child was crying. I asked her if she wanted me to call her later, but she said no, talking and changing the diaper at the same time was no big deal for her. She could talk.

"Being there for somebody. That means you have to give up part of your life," I said once we got into the interview.

"You don't give up your life because you have to be there for someone else. It doesn't mean that you forgo a life for yourself. You don't give up the outside things you do."

"Outside things like what?" I challenged her.

"Outside things like travel, like shopping."

"You don't have the money to do all that."

"I can enjoy life with Albert, with my family, I have dreams. I have hopes."

"What happens when you get older and find out that those dreams ain't nothing but dreams?"

"I'm never going to find that out," she said devilishly.

"So you think not, huh?"

"As long as I live there is always going to be hope in my dreams. Okay, okay. That's what love is. It's sort of like you love your children and when you get older you have hopes and dreams for them and as they realize those dreams you enjoy that," she said, and laughed as if she had shown me the way out of another of life's little mazes.

"Your husband is not like that. He's somewhat bitter about the way life is for black folk."

"That's the warrior. I'm not a warrior. I don't have that warrior spirit, but I understand that spirit. I can see where that comes from. Yeah, yeah."

"How about a warrior who gets his butt kicked all the time?"

She laughed. "He's still a warrior. He's right back out there fighting again. I admire that. He doesn't quit and nobody's going to make him quit."

"But what if he keeps losing?"

"But see, he will win because nobody loses forever. That's not life, because life is paradoxical—for every good there is a bad, for every loss there is a win. It has to balance out. So you can have lots and lots of losses, but somewhere down the line you're gonna win." Her voice lifted and very cheerfully accented the word *win*. "Keep fighting."

"What are you talking about?" I burst into laughter. "This is all hypothetical, but what about the warrior who keeps losing. Maybe he should just give up."

"No, you never give up. If you do, life loses its meaning. There is always something to look for, to fight for, in life, you know, something to look for, fight for, do for, be for, until you leave her."

"You got some idea why we were put here?"

"I know why I was put here." She laughed the laugh again, but somewhere in what she was saying the laugh vanished. "To do what I'm doing, un-huh."

"To change diapers for babies?"

"Yes, and there is God in every one of them," she insisted. "You got to look for it sometimes," she laughed. "But it's there. There's God in everybody."

I said to Albert: "Your wife is deep."

"Is that the word?"

"What word would you use? Wise?"

He burst out laughing. "Why don't you wait for me to come up with my word?"

"I know you're going to come up with something."

"Yeah, why don't you let me tell you what?"

"Tell me what?"

"What I think she is, based on that stuff you just told me she said?"

"Yeah."

"Give me a minute. Give me a minute." His face was beaming. "I'm gonna come up with the goddamn word."

"It's cool," he said after less than a minute. "But it ain't my way. Yeah, there's God in everybody, but I get tired of the motherfuckers in the world today. I get sick and tired, because a lot of this stuff ain't right, and it is totally unnecessary. If I get me the right kind of break, I won't deal with a lot of these people out here. A lot of this shit is fucked, and I don't know whether I want to accept that, as the condition I want to live under, for my whole life. That shit puts you in a place where certain emotions can't live. Goodness can't live."

"Can love live?"

"That's why love has to be there, because that's the only relief from it."

"So how is she like your mother? She doesn't look like your mother. You say she doesn't act like your mother. Maybe she's just Southern, deep, wise, and cool."

"Yeah, okay," he said, and then he started in on me, asking questions and comparing. He found out that I did not have a wife. We rolled back into Washington, and without saying anything he got out of his van. He came back with a bouquet of flowers. He did a little sexy dance, rolling his belly around in an insinuating way before he got back inside the van. "You reminded me," he said. "I got a good wife at home." And he laughed triumphantly, as if the flowers were a way out of another of life's little mazes.

HIP-HOP *Love*

*A*nthony "Tony" Nicholas Tyler, Tony TNT, says that love is a game, like everything else, but he knows himself to be a very serious young man. He never plays games.

He is seventeen and he wants to confront me with the truth that love does not exist, but he also feels sure he will find it one day. He is in his senior year in high school, and he wants to beat me down until I accept the truth that no one talks about love anymore.

He talks about AIDS. He talks about homeless black men, "which could be my future if I don't see it all as a game. I could get played out," he says.

"By love?" I ask.

"Among other things," he responds. We are driving in the BMW that he worked two jobs to afford. "But the cops still mess with me because they think that with this car at my age, I must be selling drugs. I could get played out by the cops."

"By love?"

"That's a concept from back in the 1950s," he says in a tone that makes love sound as outmoded as, to him, I am. "Now it's totally about something else."

"What?"

"Survival. I see everyone who looks like me involved in a struggle to survive." Now he's having the conversation that he wants to have. "Every brother I know is caught up in that, so I think your question is irrelevant."

I smile at the confrontational tone in his voice. He is a big, handsome kid—six feet three inches, 210 pounds, head shaven, Nubian fashion, earring. I know he wouldn't want me to think of him as a kid because *kid* implies that he is not ready to confront.

I don't confront. If he really thought the question was irrelevant, then he wouldn't have consented to the interview. I wouldn't be in his car taking a ride to look at the world he lives in. The world where, as he says, no one talks about love anymore.

I ask him if you have to be ba-a-a-d, hard, tough, and selfish as the Deseree song says.

He doesn't answer. He disses my question. I had noticed before that this was a habit of his. He is like many other black urban high school–age males, dropout or student, who had survived the jungle that racism had created. He was not going to let this conversation be about anything that he didn't want it to be about.

I know the statistics on this world that we are driving through in Baltimore. He recites them as if he is proud. "Homicide is the number-one killer." He is proud that he is not dead. "I could show you blocks where ten young black men have been killed in the last two years. Nationally, one in four young black men are unemployed. In here, it's three of four. Four of four. Nationally, one in four is caught in the criminal 'just us' system. In here it's one in one, in some form or another. You can't miss a beat. Your foot slips and that's your ass."

"Is that why you wear your ridge-soled hiker's boots in July?" I ask in a Mr. Peeper's voice.

He laughs. "You like those?" he says.

"They're pretty nice. What's up with you guys? The radio still plays love songs."

"That's not about love. That sets the mood for when you're bonin' a dame. That's a fantasy trip in the game."

"Have you been in love before?" I ask in a Montel Williams, talk-show-host voice.

"Nah." He's caught the joke but he doesn't want to stay with it.

"Do you want to be in love?" I ask slowly, giving him time to decide whether he is going to pursue this line of conversation or dis my question again.

"Yeah."

"You do?" I try to sound like his second-grade teacher. I know he doesn't like this talk-show, schoolteacher shit, but I'm not going to make his job of convincing easy.

"Uh-huh."

"Why?"

"I don't know."

"Even if a chick breaks your heart, wouldn't you want to see what it's like?"

"You gotta take risks, take a risk in everything you do."

"Would you rather date somebody that was your friend or meet somebody?"

"A friend," he says sullenly.

"So, then, friendship is very important to you," I say, staying corny to see how much corniness he will take against the backdrop of disaster rolling outside the window.

"Yeah."

"Do you date a lot of people at one time?"

"No."

"Not searching?"

"It is not necessarily a matter of searching or not searching. It all depends on how much you trust that person you're with. If you know that the one person you're with won't cheat on you, then I won't do that to her. But if I'm in the kind of relationship where this girl sees the opportunity and she meets somebody else, then I'll do the same. But that's not it. That's not it," he says in frustration.

I know that that's not it. I know that there are so many things for a young guy to avoid, psychological traps. In this neighborhood everyone his age has children, no one goes to school, no one does anything, so they think that's normal. No role models. Most of the youngsters don't think that there's anything wrong with that life-style.

People selling drugs, a continuous cycle. Staying in school has required a lot of TNT. It has taken a lot to keep his head above water. Some of the guys his age claim that he is "losing his black-ness" by trying to be something in life.

"We don't talk about love. If you have that look, you're com-fortable, you have a decent amount of money, or I've got a car, I know how to dress. Women have been taught it's all about eco-nomics," he says, trying forcefully to get me to see that it's not about love.

"It's about how much money they got, how many cars they got, that's what makes a man. So the guy with nothing on the ball, he gives a girl money, and he knocks her down, and that's how it goes. She's not going anywhere as long as he has that money. She might say she loves him. Girl thinks she's playing a guy out. She's playing herself out. An ugly four-foot dude in a beemer [BMW], he knows the beemer is why that girl is with him. He's not dumb."

"Is it just material? There's nothing else you see?" We talk about materialism.

"I'm always careful if a girl's out for my car or if she's out for me. Because a friend is not like that. A friend is a friend regardless. I never juiced a girl for her money. I'm not like that, but on the other hand, how do I know if a girl likes me for me or likes me because of my car? How can you know for sure?"

"You got a nice car. You're a nice-looking guy. It could be both."

"So I don't need to tell if a bitch is with me for me or with me for my car. Let's say, for instance, you meet somebody, and you know she likes you for your car. So, do you see it as her driving around in your car? You get whatever you get from her, do you see it as both getting taken advantage of? Or do you see it as you taking advantage of her?

"So there's the wife of the white doctor driving out on the highway in her Mercedes that he bought. Does she love him for him or does she love him because of the Mercedes, the house, the vacations, et cetera, et cetera, et cetera. It's all the same thing.

"She loves him for both. Now suppose this girl says, 'I don't love him for his car, but the only reason he has the nerve to step to a girl who looks like me is because he has such and such car, such and such money.' It's still the same thing—materialism. It's a game.

"If I drive past, whatever, and she just keeps her face in order, at that little point, she saw the car. You get out and she sees you later, then she can say she's after you and not your car because then she can say she just happens to notice all the wonderful qualities you have, but that was because she saw you in the car first and told herself that she didn't notice the car."

"What qualities do you look for in a woman?" I ask to keep him from getting tangled up in his own urgency.

"When I first see a girl, of course, the first thing you see is her looks. It's all physical, no doubt about that. It's definitely what she looks like that counts. When you're young that's what it is. It's in the face. How cute is her face? But also it's in her sex appeal—you check the buttocks, the legs, the breast—the overall sexiness."

I decide to throw a wringer into his monologue too. "It's not all in the looks, is it?"

"When it starts off, that's all it can be about. What else do you have to go on?"

"So you're looking to get the best combination of face and body you can get?" I ask.

"And so is she and she's also looking for a car thrown in."

"What do you want thrown in?"

"Self-respect, intelligence. One thing I can't stand is a ditz. I can't stand girls that can't think for themselves. When I sit back and have a conversation with them, I gotta be able to sit down and have an intellectual conversation with them."

"But you didn't select her based on her potential to do that."

"To do what?"

"To have an intellectual conversation. You selected her for looks and now you want her to have . . ."

"I didn't say I selected her for looks, that's the first reason I started checking her out. That's what I mean when I say 'start talking to a girl.' I give them . . . I treat that person better than I treat most girls. That's how she knows I'm checking her out. I start to give her more attention, in most cases, or else I can come right out and tell her that I'm checking her out.

"A lot of times I can come out and just say it. I'm not scared when it comes to certain people, I don't know . . . certain girls I just can't approach. It all depends on the situations. If you and this person is real, real, real cool, then you can approach that person anyway because you're casual, you're not worried about her thinking that you're sweatin' her."

"*Sweatin' her* means you're on her case, checking her out?" I ask.

"It depends. I can't explain it to you. It depends on the type of relationship you have and how long you've had a relationship. Today we call ourselves cool, tomorrow if I started to like you, it would be easier for me to tell you I like you tomorrow than it would be in six months.

"Then you have to worry about what the outcome of the friendship will be, because if I had told you right away that I was checking you out, then there would have been no friendship to mess up."

"You know what I think?"

"Naw."

"I think that you feel that friendship is more important than love."

"Why would you say that?"

"Because you sound like you'd be more worried about messing up a friendship than messing up a love."

"Yeah, because the friendship is something you already have. The love is something you're hoping to have. How can you mess up something you don't have yet. What's the loss? I'm just saying that love changes quicker than friendship. People think going with somebody is all lovey-dovey and it has to be all this and all that, and I think that's why love relationships don't work out, because you're basing it all on sensual feelings and stuff like that and that's not what love is about.

"To me love means an understanding between two people, where they're out for each other, and they want the best for each other. They care for each other in a genuine way, you know, their relationship is not one-sided. It's not what you can get from me, it's what you can do, stuff like that.

"If you give me a chance, and if it's the woman I want, then our relationship can be so-called ideal. I'm flexible, I have a lot of respect for women, because of my upbringing, and I have a lot of respect for myself."

"Then, you do believe in love. What you just said proves that."

"It doesn't prove that there is such a thing in the world. Okay, suppose I talk to you about ghosts. I can talk to you for half an hour about ghosts, but do they exist? You tell me. You show me one."

Earlier TNT had said he had to have the car or the guys who sold reefer would have the best shots at the best-looking honeys in the city. So after school three nights a week he works in a doctor's office.

He likes when Dr. Baker's wife comes in. She is a pretty brown-skinned woman with a nice build. "Fine," he has told his buddies at the barbershop on numerous occasions. He brags that he thinks she likes him. "I'd like to hit it once or twice," he has said.

He has watched, hoping that she doesn't really love Dr. Baker, he's said. He says he hopes this because he would like to hit it one time, if she ever gave him the chance.

The doctor's office is the one place of order in TNT's life. He likes the smell of it as he does the filing assigned to him, and if everyone else is busy he might check a blood pressure. He has thought about being a doctor.

Sometimes there in the waiting room he sees something that might be love—a couple might be there, and from the way they act there might be a chance that they love each other. Once in a while there are cases that seem like love—a woman and man joking with or comforting each other.

But much more often the man or the woman waits with the other as if he or she does not want to be there. Sometimes both are like that and he cannot tell if it is the stress of the medical problem or the stress of their being together that fills the air around them with tension.

Mothers scream at children, trying to make them behave. One of the nurses, Marcia, might be going with Dr. Baker. Anthony is suspicious. Marcia is fine—dark-skinned, stacked, in white uniform, white panty hose, and makeup. Anthony watches because he wants to know what love and life are really like "in the real world," as he calls the doctor's world.

"More than love, I would consider: is this a good person for me to be around. That's why I would say somebody who is smart, has self-respect for themselves, knows how to treat herself, knows how to treat a guy, won't let me get away with anything and won't try to get away with anything with me—a girl who forces me to respect her,'' he says the day after I met him at the doctor's office.

"Why does she have to force you?"

"Because you can't respect everybody, because not everybody deserves respect. A woman has to demand respect. Especially in these days. A man has to demand respect from a woman. She would earn more and more respect from me as time went by."

"How?"

"Just little things she does."

"Like what, do you mean?"

"Okay, take for example, we could be on the phone or whatever and she's asking me . . . like, there's a report I have to do. Let's say I'm with her and there's a report I have to do and she's, like, well . . . 'I'd rather you do the report than spend time with me.' You respect that person more and more, and when I find out she's not selfish and she's out for my best interest, which is telling me to do the school report, or the other homework, you just keep rolling with her or just roll on.

"Because it's the little things she does that're going to influence you. Just like your family members influence you—your girlfriend influences you—your girlfriend is another extension of your family. They're all relationships. Anybody you're with for a certain period of time will influence you, whether it's positive or negative.

"But we don't talk about love, per se. Come by the barbershop tomorrow, and I'll show you," he says. "I'll prove it to you."

TNT is determined to make his point. He knows that a barbershop in a ghetto is no place to take me to make me see. The barbershop where he works his second job sits in an old, small, rundown shopping center on Spreewell Avenue near where Route 40 changes from being a local street into a freeway.

During the week only old dudes are there with Anthony barbering. Their conversations sometimes contain clues about how love has treated them over the years. However, most of all, love is something they *accuse* each other of, as if it is a game that one or another of them has lost.

Fifty Jones was accused of it for my benefit, just to see what he would say. He neither confirmed nor denied it. He simply didn't answer. His nonanswer allowed him to be the butt of the joke about this thing called love, that any of them could fall victim to in their efforts to find "someone to stick their dicks into," as Fifty says.

It is a hot day in July. Fifty allows himself to be the butt of the slow-paced jokes about love as the four other barbers ponder the question: "What is love in the 1990s?"

Meanwhile, Fifty Jones enjoys being the butt of the jokes. He is a handsome man. He could well have been a lover back before he picked up the nickname "Fifty." He seems happy that the others are implying that he is still a lover at his age. The name Fifty must have been given to him fifteen years ago, because he is about sixty-five now, but Sixty-Five Jones is not as good as Fifty Jones.

When the other barbers get him cornered on whether it was his abilities as a lover or his abilities at oral sex that made him popular with the women, he takes to his own defense: "Only God can love. The rest of us just try. We try but we can't really love or else there wouldn't be all of this lust, greed, jealousy, envy, divorce, fighting, lying, killing, people scheming and plotting on each other. A human being can approach love, but he can't get there," he says. He has fought the others off him.

"But what about oral sex," one of the other barbers asks.

"He's not talking about agape, he's talking about Eros," one of the other barbers says, referring to me, who had asked the original question.

"What you're talking about is agape, the love that God gives to mankind. He's talking about Eros, which comes from the Greek word *Eros,* which refers to the love between a man and a woman," the other barber says, to show that Fifty is not the only smart person in the shop.

"Greek love means anal intercourse, that's what it means," says one of the other barbers.

"Now you're moving down Fifty's alley. You know why Buster comes in here, don't you?" another barber says, and points his comb at Fifty.

I assume that Buster is a homosexual. There are several who hang out in the shopping center.

Anthony takes it all in. He is pleased that I am hearing it. The barbers are "getting his point across," which seems to be the goal of his life, getting his point across.

He tells me to come back on the weekend and just sit. I can pick the guy, no matter who it is, and no matter what guy I pick the guy will prove his point. The guy will not talk about love.

The young barbers come in on Fridays and Saturdays because they can give the fades, baldies, flat tops, Caesar's, temple tapers, or monogram cuts that the young weekend customers like. I am there at about three in the hot afternoon. The place is air-conditioned. I watch to see who I'd like to talk to. Most of the guys who come in are older than Anthony. They range from the mid-twenties to mid-forties or so. The guys in the mid-forties are considered young guys because of the way they carry themselves.

One of the guys who has come in, a light-skinned guy with dreadlocks, is obviously a hip-hop deejay because he talks about setting up his turntables for a hip-hop party that night. I nod to TNT, indicating that I want to interview the deejay, whose name, I learn, is "Yellow Nubian" or "Yellow Yellow."

"Hey, Yellow Yellow, this dude is writing a book on love. I been trying to tell him that we don't talk about love, in our generation. Would you tell him?"

TNT seems not at all ashamed that he has already indicated to Yellow Yellow what he wanted Yellow Yellow to say. TNT has already biased the interview. Yellow Yellow takes a long look at me.

He takes the floor. "Attitude is, let's say, not so seriously taken, not seriously taken on love, and I don't know if, coming from my age range, a lot of the kids know what love is—it's lust, lust for something material, something momentary."

TNT purses his lips and shakes his head up and down. It is as if these two cats have gotten their vibes together and now they are in perfect sync with each other. It's a double-team. I try to break it up by sounding more like a professor than I do in a classroom. "When I look through music," I say, and pause to slow the game down to my pace. "I looked through some soul lyrics at the Library of Congress a lot." Everybody in the barbershop is listening to my alien tone. "The rappers, the rap singers, the rap musicians, the hip-hop guys, they mention love."

"Right, there's always a love for something material. There's that. There's always that. That seems to be . . . what you just said sums it up. Because it's about cars, the clothes, jewelry.

"I would say exactly that. It's about the material things. I would say at this age, it's like a cycle, you're not gonna love that girl or get that girl to love you if you don't get a car or have what she needs." Yellow Nubian is good. He has taken what I said and passed it back to TNT.

TNT purses his lips again and shakes his head up and down.

"I see it as trying to keep up with the Willies, the Big Willies, and the Big Wilmas and the Big Mommas. And the ladies . . . there's a lyric that would twist your head if you heard it."

There is nothing I can do now but enjoy the show. I throw out a comment, but I know they have run the fast break past me. "But the word *love* is used in some of the songs."

Yellow Nubian takes my comment again and deflects it toward TNT. "This song has the word *love* in it, but it is so vulgar. I'm not sure what the title is, but it just came out a few weeks ago. But it doesn't get played on daytime radio, but it gets played on college overnight after-twelve radio. And the record is so vulgar, there's no love in the record, there's love for material item and that's it." He has slam-dunked.

TNT is happy. Without looking at him Yellow Nubian comes and stands over me.

"Vulgar, you mean in terms of sex acts?" I have to say something. I can't let him stand over me and me not say anything.

"Right, and what I'm also saying is to be so vulgar you don't really love this person or that person or anything other than money and all the things that money can bring. It is really that cut and dry."

I know he is feeling around for what TNT might want him to say next. "And the woman's verse is so vulgar that you can see why the guy would have to chase this material chain to make possible for the girl." He has found TNT. TNT purses his lips and shakes his head up and down. Yellow Nubian does not have to look at him. He knows.

"It's not a love thing for him or her, it's about . . . I would even say, that song "You're All I Need," the Marvin Gaye record they did over, it's kinda . . . the love in that record is drawn from a need to have everything we want in life, or it comes from a need that comes from a lack."

He's got me now. The word *lack* put him in his own conversation. We are all now listening to him because he is serious.

"A need for love or lack of love, it's a lack of everything you want in love and wanting to have everything, including love, to share it with something. It's just not the record that says I love you and expresses that. It says, 'You're all I need. I don't have anything else, there's nothing else, but I want to get this foundation for us to live on and have this money in the bank and you're all I need to get there.'

"It's not exactly enough to say 'I love you and you're all I need to make it through,' but 'You're all I need to get by to get there.' I think from a young age, a slightly-younger-than-me standpoint, it's very easy to say these are the things we want and need— not just the love, we need what is necessary to get us through. The love and the honesty, and the faith in this to get us through, but it's a lack of what we have and their positive love side to see what we want to see." He stops.

"Okay," I say.

I come back to the barbershop when TNT's shift is over at ten-thirty P.M. I wanted to finish up my interview on love. He is happy that Fifty Jones and Yellow Nubian confirmed his statement that nobody talks about love anymore.

In fact, that was the first thing he said as we walked to his car. "I told you nobody talks about love, as, per se, 'I love you.' 'I love her.' 'She loves me.' "

"What do you say?" I ask as we get in his car.

"What do you mean?"

"About girls? Do you call them 'bitches'? 'My bitch.' 'My ho.' "

"No, not necessarily. You might say 'my girl.' 'My stuff.' "

"So how do you go about falling in love with 'stuff,' since you don't fall in love, finding you some stuff? Is there a special place you hang out when you want to get into some stuff? Or do you just wait until you just happen to meet the stuff of your life.''

"It's not something you're looking for. It's something you're looking forward to, but it's not something you're looking for. It'll happen. It'll happen. It just happens.''

"So you don't think there's a specific time when you want it to happen, when you want to be in a relationship?''

"No, every time is a best time.''

"Have you ever dated some stuff and you look back and say, 'No, I shouldn't have dated her?' ''

"Yeah, everybody I dated, so far . . . well, not everybody, but most of the people. Most definitely.'' He was comfortable now that he had won the interview game. The conversation was going as he had wanted it to go in the first place. He had beaten me down.

"What about abusing your stuff. Have you ever mistreated or taken advantage of somebody?''

"Well, not if I wasn't taken advantage of. A woman knows that I'll accept so much. I'm very cool and she might think she can play me out.''

"How?''

"You know, you might want to be their everything. You might not want them going to places, especially when she's a real attractive dame. You might have to play her out first.''

"Why?''

"Okay, take for example, when she's going to be in an environment where she might meet somebody. You don't want her looking at these other guys, or maybe he has a bad car. It could be anything like that.''

"Or you might cheat on her.''

"I would think . . . yeah, if I see another woman. You say, 'Sure, go ahead.' I mean, if she's not better than what you've got, it's not going anywhere anyway, so the same is true of her. It depends on the connection you have with her.

"But she might hear about some girl riding in your car, but nothing's happening. You're just giving that girl a ride, checking her out, but you're not pushing up on her.

"Or it might not be you. It might be her. She just might want to get up in your face. I think the problem is a woman might think she has your heart and so she feels she can do anything she wants, 'cause you ain't going nowhere. She has your heart.

"Then, when you start showing them you're able to go, that's when they want to change. They want to hold on to you and all that stuff."

"As their stuff."

"Precisely. But as soon as it gets to that point, I don't want to deal with it anymore. That's when they start wanting me more, more and more, and that just pushes me away."

"Okay."

"I really don't know. That's what I can't stand about women. Women want you when you don't want them. That's the problem. And they want you more and more and you really don't want them."

"So you're saying that if you'd fall in love she would stop treating you well?"

"I notice, when it starts, she couldn't treat me any better, but after a while, hold on, wait a second, don't flip the script, because we're in a serious relationship and you know you have my heart, don't just all of a sudden decide you can just say things and give me no respect just because you know you have my heart."

"When did you learn all this?" I ask.

"What?" he asks.

"All of this."

"I knew this by the time I was thirteen."

Love IN A DREAM HOUSE

*B*ill says that he loves his wife, Tanya, but that he's "not *in* love *with* Tanya, how-so-ever we can't get a divorce because then I'd have to sell the house."

It is easy enough for someone like me, who has never owned or lived in a house like Bill's, to ask: "Why don't you sell it? Why stay in a relationship just because of a house? Why be miserable because of a house? Why not sell the house and split the equity so that everybody can go their separate ways?"

Bill says: "What good would that do? Go where? I don't have anyone else that I want to spend my life with. I'm not miserable," he says. As we drive north on Connecticut's Merritt Parkway in his beautiful green Land Rover, Bill seems, in fact, a very cheerful man, a happy marketeer for a Fortune 500 company.

A white woman named Connie Brisco, from Atlanta, Georgia, who worked for Bill during what their company calls "the Chicago Miracle," says: "Bill Carter is the best natural marketeer I have seen in my twenty years in management at four different hard-charging, sales-oriented companies. It is a pleasure to work for this man."

Bill does not admit to being materialistic. In fact, he says, "I've always considered myself an incurable romantic. I'm a romantic sort of person, but until I find the right person to romance and for the right reasons, it sort of sits on the shelf until I decide to pull it down and use it." He laughs. The sunlit woodland moves smoothly by outside the Land Rover.

I had seen his house before and I thought of love sitting on one of the shelves in it. The house itself is a series of three shelves, or pyramidal tiers, jutting out of the side of a rocky hill in Connecticut not far from Stamford, where Bill works as a marketing vice president in what is called corporate America.

The tiers are enclosed mostly by floor-to-ceiling glass panels, so that the wilderness outside is a part of the decor. There are shelves in the two room-sized closets in the master bedroom suite, but his romantic nature wouldn't be there, because the master bedroom suite is where his wife sleeps.

"She's a control freak, so she wanted the master bedroom, okay, because of the title. And because it sits by itself on the top tier overlooking everything. But actually, the guest suite has a blue marble tile bathroom, with a blue whirlpool, which I love.

"From the bathroom in the guest suite there is a stairway down to the spa, which contains a sauna. The suite has two bedrooms, and so I can use one of them as my office without even going outside the suite." He laughs without a hint of bitterness.

There is no reason for bitterness. Life, to him, is a game. He is in the part of the game called love, and he has the sense that he is winning. Or, rather, love is like the fierce competition between business firms, and he feels that he has the most successful business plan.

"The master suite has a total of about eleven hundred square feet. The guest suite has a total of twenty-two hundred square feet." He makes a palms-up gesture and shrugs his shoulders and laughs. "Twice the size. Almost exactly twice the size."

"You're still married?" I ask, even though I think I know the answer.

"Our marriage is in an arrangement sort of setting. We were about to get a divorce and my biggest concern was that I had bought the house before I got married, so at the time that the divorce-type situation came up I had some concerns that I would have to sell the house to pay her her portion of the divorce settlement.

"I had a concern about that so the day before the final hearing our lawyers struck an agreement that she would not pursue the divorce and property settlement if I would submit to counseling to try to keep the marriage together, and at the same time an agreement was signed off on that my wife would reduce the size of her demand in the property settlement if I still decided to go through with the divorce after two years of counseling."

"Two years?"

"Yeah, two years. She wanted five years," he screams.

"That's behavior modification."

"Tell me about it."

"So the decision to remain married was not based on love? Was the decision to get married based on love?"

"I love her, but I'm not in love with her from the romantic standpoint. I'm not there. I was there, but I'm not there at this particular time," he says. He laughs.

"Two years of counseling should get it back for you," I say sarcastically. I have judged by now that he is not offended by sarcasm or much else that comes at him.

"I want to get that back. I want to be in love. I wouldn't have a problem being in love with her. We've had some good times and some bad times, okay. But she has some ways about her that are somewhat very stifling.

"For example, a week ago I was making a sandwich in the kitchen, okay. I had all the stuff out on the counter to make my sandwich. The phone rang and I went to the phone in the living room and she came down and put away all of the things that I had out."

"Just to annoy you?"

"Naw, naw, naw, I wish it was. Naw, she is the kind who

thinks you should take the bread out and put two pieces on your plate, and then put the bread back in the bread box; take the mayonnaise out, spread some on the bread, and put it back in the refrigerator; take the mustard out, use it, and put it back; take the tomato out, slice it, put the slices on the bread, wrap it in cellophane, and put it back; then take the lettuce out—one at a time."

"Damn."

"Oh, yeah!"

"And I'm a person like this: I like to take everything out at once and make my sandwich. I was pissed. I am a free-willed type of person. I like to have fun. I like to laugh. Her thing is you only laugh twice a week. She likes order. We're talking about an anal retentive here. I'm not finished making my sandwich—hel-lo-o-o." He acts as if he is peeping under his wife's blindfold to see if there is a brain inside her head. "Is anybody home?"

I could see why the guy was regarded as one of the best marketeers in corporate America. He could work with anything and make it funny.

"It's just clean-up, after clean-up, after clean-up, in addition to what the housekeeper does. The housekeeper makes the place spotless, but if I come into the house and take my coat off and lay it across a chair for a minute, I guarantee you that she will get up right then and put the coat on a hanger and put it in the closet. All of that is not necessary."

We finally get to the house where we had spent the night before in the office of his suite looking at a basketball game on television. His wife had been in the house, up on her tier. I had seen her get out of her Mercedes in the driveway, but I had not met her. He didn't want me to meet her because he had concerns about how candid he could be if she and her lawyer knew he was being interviewed on the subject of love.

We park the Land Rover in the driveway, leaving enough room

for her to get her Mercedes into the two-car garage. "You don't put your car in the garage just to piss her off?" I ask.

"Naw, it's not going to rain. Why should I put it in the garage?"

The house is magnificent. I remember the tour he took me on the night before. The tile in the bathrooms and kitchen gleamed almost as if the rooms had never been used. The huge living room opened onto a vast patio that made the outdoors part of the living space on each of the tiers.

He told me he had bought the house in 1978 after he made a lot of money back in the mid-1970s, when the company was giving out huge bonuses for performance. The company had put him in as branch manager in Chicago, which was number ten in the company. "Chicago! Number ten!" he had screamed.

He moved the Chicago branch to number one in three years. "Ahead of New York!" He slapped the palm of his right hand with the back of his left hand. "Ahead of Washington!" He slapped the palm of his left hand with the back of his right hand. "Ahead of Los Angeles!" He threw both palms up as if there were nothing left to say.

He had said the company loved him so much that he was moved to corporate headquarters in Stamford and given a huge bonus, which he used for the down payment on the house.

The company arranged a 5 percent mortgage on the $300,000 balance of the $567,000 purchase price. "At the height of the real estate boom this house was worth two million dollars. It may not be worth that much now, but it's worth more than that to me."

"You're a romantic? Incurable?"

"Yup." He leans his head to the side. "Do you see a problem with that definition? If you see a problem, tell me."

"Naw, no problem. I want to ask the same question: So the decision to remain married was not based on love? Was the decision to get married based on love?"

"Define love."

"For the sake of the book we are defining love as *my dictionary* defines it. Love is: one, an intense affectionate concern for another person; and two, an intense sexual desire for another person."

"Which one of those definitions do your doubts pertain to?" He tilts his head to the side again, waiting.

"Why did you two get married?"

"Love, and the love of a challenge, and my wife has many qualities that would enhance a very successful package. Let me tell you how I got together with Tanya.

"You know I was in Chicago, right. I was the first African-American branch manager in the company and they gave me the toughest branch, okay, typical. I didn't complain because a problem is an opportunity in disguise."

"Okay, I heard of the Chicago Miracle."

"Right. Well, I was out of the branch for about three years. I was regional manager, northeast region, and I got the 411 and the 911 that there was this fine, hot-shot new sales rep out of New York City who had just been hired in my old branch in Chicago.

"There aren't that many black sales reps in the company, so news travels fast and this was hot. She was putting up fantastic sales numbers and I kept getting calls on her from white folk and black folk.

"They were telling her that she had to meet me. They were telling me that I had to meet her. Sooner or later we have to meet. I talked to her a few times on the phone and she admitted that she had heard a lot about me. I admitted I had heard a lot about her.

"Corporate America for black folk at our level is a very small circle, and so news gets around from company to company and within a company, especially. It's a by-product of serious networking. The network provides channels for gossip too.

"Of course she knew I could do a lot of good things to help

her career, and also there was the competitive element. I was hot. She was hot.

"She was fresh in the company and fresh in corporate America, and so none of the guys had had her, and I wanted to get cracking before someone else made the move.

"I began talking to her almost daily on the phone. It all sounded good. I had some of my boys in the Chicago branch check her out. She wouldn't date anybody in the company. She said she was waiting for me.

"Finally, I sent her this ticket to come in to corporate headquarters so we could meet. Before she came I had gone down to New York in the East Fifties to this Italian tailor and gotten a new suit especially for the day she was to come in.

"She flew into La Guardia and took a limo up to Stamford. I made sure I was out of my office when she got there, and I had my secretary seat her in my office, with all the sales trophies and plaques I had won.

"I came back and talked to my secretary just outside the office where I could see Tanya through the door. I could see her legs, and I swear, she had the greatest pair of legs east of the Mississippi, or, what is Chicago? West of the Mississippi? Whatever. She had great legs.

"Then I went into the office and saw the rest of her. I never saw a neater package in my life. I don't mean with makeup. It was a clean look. Nothing was out of place. I didn't know it then, but this was going to be one of the problems, but when I first saw her, I was in love.

"You say that there's nothing such as love at first sight. What was that definition of love you gave?" he asks.

"*My dictionary* says love is: one, an intense affectionate concern for another person; and two, an intense sexual desire for another person."

"Okay, sitting there in my office—beautiful hair, perfect teeth, perfectly clean peach-colored skin, nice smile—was my intense affectionate concern and certainly my intense sexual desire. We talked. Neither one of us was giving much ground. We were both ba-a-a-d.

"That evening I had a limo pick her up at the Greenwich Marriott Hotel, where we had put her up, and bring her to the house. I know she was impressed but she couldn't afford to say so, but you know what impressed her most?"

"What?"

"I was in an apron when she arrived. I can cook. I learned intentionally because one of the things that always would get me where I needed to go, in terms of relationships, is the fact that I can cook.

"I have this fabulous house and I can cook. Regardless of what the objective was, if the objective was to turn somebody on and then drop them off, or if the objective was to have a relationship.

"I can cook and that to me is very romantic. I knew she was coming in, and so I was going to have a meal for her and all. She came and walked into the house and, this was before anything sexual had taken place, she said, 'Um-m-m, something smells good.'

"I said to myself, 'I'm in. It's on.' You know what I'm saying? 'It's on.' That simple remark let me know. They say that food is a way to a man's heart. It gets to a woman's heart faster.

"In fact, a woman is more impressed with a man who can cook well than a man is with a woman who can cook well, because it's expected. I had fixed some bluefish the way the West Indians cook it, and some Uncle Ben's rice. It was slammin'." He goes wild. He's the happiest I have seen him all during this happy day. "It was slammin'.

"So we got it on and we started this long-distance relationship. She said she wasn't seeing anybody. I think she was telling the truth. But unless you're sitting in someone else's panties, or in someone else's drawers, you never know, but I think she was telling the truth.

"She knew I was seeing somebody, but I didn't think she knew I was seeing some bodies. I was a bachelor, making a lot of money, interacting with a lot of attractive single ladies inside the company and out, so my dance card was filled."

"Was there anyone special before her?"

"They all were special," he says, sidestepping the trap I am laying for him. "There was nobody super-duper special. They all knew about her. Some of them even knew when I was engaged to her.

"I can't recall the exact moment when we decided to get engaged, but we dated long-distance for over eighteen months. I would fly out to Chicago, or, most often, she would fly in to New York, because she has folks in New York.

"For my part it was time for me to get married. I had told myself that I would be married by twenty-five, and here I was, knock, knock, knocking on thirty-five. It was time."

"Then, it was a scheduling thing," I say, to see if I could convince him that many people would not regard him as an incurable romantic.

"It wasn't just a scheduling thing. There was romance involved. For example, I proposed to her on the beach at sunset in Malibu, in California. We had had romantic trips to Hawaii, to Cancun, so it was definitely a romantic sort of thing, but love doesn't have to be blind."

"Have you ever been just blindly in love?"

"No, I have never been blindly in nothing. My mother said I was born with my eyes wide open. I had been in love before, oh yeah. A fair amount, but never really blind."

"I never had been engaged before, or was I? I remember one

who I might have been engaged to. I know I had talked about marriage with this one woman. Let's put it this way. I don't think I'd ever bought an engagement ring, that I can remember.

"Anyway, I'm never blindly in love. I have a set of requirements before the romance even starts. I like a woman I can have a conversation with. I don't need to talk to myself. I've heard myself before. Education is important—formal education—but I also want someone who's bright.

"I know folks who went to school just to get their MRS degree, you know, 'Misiz' degree, so to speak. They just went to get a degree and get a man who had a degree also.

"I like for them to know what's going on in the world. There's only about one woman I've been in love with who was not attuned to politics, business, and things of that nature. Because I stay up on that. You start talking about Bosnia. You start talking about Cuba. You start talking about bills that are going through the House and Senate.

"I can have conversations about that. Male and female, black or white, I like to be around people who can handle those types of conversation. Maybe I'm weird in that standpoint, but I've always liked current events.

"Most of the women I had been involved with up to that point could get involved in conversations like this. I should have noticed that Tanya never talked about any of this. But the current events. That's not a big drawback for me, okay. It's sorta like an added bonus.

"She might have known about current events, because she was educated, but the only thing she talked about was 'the game,' me and her and how we could put what we had together and create a synergy that would be greater than the total of what we had separately.

"I was very much in love, you could say. Let me tell you what she did. If I wasn't in love, or blinded by love, you could say I would have reacted to this in a way that would have meant that we would never have gotten married.

"While we were engaged, somehow she had gotten my Rolodex out of my office, okay, without me knowing it, or even noticing that it had been gone, and she had taken all of the cards out of it containing women's names, and she had made a computerized list of them, and she had put beside each name one of three classifications: 'legitimate business,' 'personal,' and 'monkey business.' She presented me with this list. I was livid. 'This ain't none of your business.'

Even when he is recalling being livid, he can laugh. I have to laugh too. His wife-to-be had pulled a pretty good trick, and she must have known him enough to know that he would not call the marriage off, that he would like the challenge.

"She is somewhat of a control freak. She wanted me to clean my Rolodex of all 'monkey business.' All former female friends had to go."

"Did they go?"

"No."

"Have they gone?"

"No, but it was her. Of all of the women I knew, she was the one I wanted to marry. She was perfect. She could, of course, mix and mingle in the company. She loved that, or in corporate settings in general. I was very proud of her because in those circles she was a star.

"It didn't bother me that she was competitive. I like competitive people. You can't have a hard-charger in a company who isn't competitive. Tanya was striving to do more, to further herself and all.

"I do remember one case when I had this woman who couldn't mingle. I used to take her to company social functions. Very pretty lady, but she sounded like a Mouseketeer—'hel-lo-o-o, hel-lo-o-o.' This was during the time of airhead-dipitus, you know. So someone, go get a pump so we can pump some more air into her. 'Hel-lo-o-o.'

"You can excuse some of the wives for sounding like that. Okay, that's what that is, but I always enjoyed having a woman who could draw respect. Tanya—boom. She was perfect.

"I was the one who got her transferred to Stamford. I was the one who sent her back to law school, even before we were married. I did that. She had been to law school before she came into the company and hadn't finished, so I helped her get back into law school.

"I'm a person like this: I'm very generous, but I like being around people. She doesn't care for people, unless it's in a formal type, career-advancing setting."

"What did you like about being married?"

"It was actually fun to turn her out, sexually. That was a gas. I enjoyed that tremendously. She is the kind of person, when we are having sex she likes to be in control. I enjoyed overriding her control.

"The way things operate, in terms of sex, have a good time, this is not about control. When it's time to come, you just come. Now, she complained that I was not like that, that I liked to control when I came.

"I had to control because on a nightly basis, I'm a one-trick pony. If I come once, that's it for me in the space of the kind of time I have to spend on a weeknight when I have to get up in the morning.

"With her she has a problem. She doesn't want to—quote, unquote—lose it, and it's like, girl, I wish I could do like you do. You can have multiorgasms. You can come ten or fifteen times.

"Just orgasm after orgasm after orgasm. I remember this one time, and maybe this took something out of it, but I counted how many orgasms this woman could have. One time she had fifteen orgasms, and it's not that I'm saying that I'm that good.

"In terms of lovemaking, I'm the kind of person who's interested in learning what turns the other person on. I look at it like this: if I can turn this woman on, if I can make her have an orgasm, or multiorgasms, I'll be invited back again. I will be invited back into the party, you know. What's that song that Michael Henderson sings? He says that once he's been there he can always go back. I'm like that.'

"I don't think that sex is the most important thing. It's like oil. Oil is a necessary ingredient to keep the vehicle running. It's not as important as the engine. Sex is not the engine, but if you don't have that oil, sooner or later you're going to ruin the engine. Sex is like the oil.''

I decided to try to sum up what he had said: "Marriage is like the engine; sex is the oil that keeps the engine humming?''

"No. Sex is the oil, love is the engine. Marriage is the car you're both riding in. The marriage license is the title to ownership of the car,'' he laughs.

"By the time you got married had you sorted out all your monkey business?''

"Yes, and no. As far as she was concerned, yes; as far as I was concerned, no. I tried to clean everything up, but there was still something I had to do. Two weekends after we came back from our honeymoon, I had to fly out to the West Coast to do something one last time for the Gipper. Good-bye fun, but for a year after that I was faithful.''

"So right after the honeymoon someone was driving her car?''

"No. I wasn't married to this other lady. I was just taking a spin in a car I used to own.'' He laughs.

"How long have you been married?''

"Nine years—1987 to 1996.''

"Has she ever caught you fucking up?''

"I mean yes. I mean at various times. I remember she flew into Washington, D.C., and caught me in a hotel with another woman, but I was separated at the time. I was trying to sue the hotel because she said they had told her that I had reserved a suite for two. Hotels are not supposed to give out information like that.

"Anyway, she flew in to National Airport in the afternoon, coolly took care of some company business, and then came by my hotel at three in the morning. She had her clown suit on. She was ready to clown.

"She got a key to the room by showing that she was Mrs. William Carter. The hotel didn't know she wasn't staying in the room, so they gave her a key.

"She came into the room and sat down while me and this woman were in bed. 'What the fuck is this?' She said: 'Why are you here? Do you love her?' 'Why are you here?' She stayed for over an hour. She and the woman started calling each other names. I thought they were going to start boxing. They woke up the entire hotel. They had to call hotel security."

I try not to laugh, but pretty soon I break and then he breaks.

"But hotel security couldn't say who should be put out of the room." He reaches over, touches me on the arm, and brings me into the story. We are both laughing. "Tanya said that she had a right to be in the room since the room was rented to Mr. and Mrs. Bill Carter. 'I'm Mrs. Bill Carter. I don't know who this other person is in my room.' See, she had her clown suit on. She had come there ready to clown."

"You gotta admit she was putting on a good show," I say.

"Yeah, yeah, yeah, she was clowning."

I am laughing so hard that tears start coming from my eyes. He is a marvel of unemotionality.

"Wait a minute," he says. "Wait a minute. Wait. She said, 'Get this ugly little thing out of my room.' The other woman was a Xerox sales manager. She's scrambling around getting her clothes together. . . ." He gets up and pretends to be a half-naked woman scurrying to get her clothes together while holding a wig in place. Bill Carter is funny.

"Tanya was cool. It was almost as if she was complaining about bad room service. She got the room-service people to change the sheets on the bed and she crawled up in the bed and went to sleep. To sleep! Amazing."

"Did you stop seeing this other woman?"

"No, because basically it wasn't none of Tanya's damn business. We were separated at the time. You know, one of those things. You go your way and I'll go mine. This is what she had told me. This is what we had agreed on, but then later she said: 'If I ever see you with another woman, it is my civic duty to tell her what a horrible person you are.' She said, 'I am appointing myself as a one-woman truth squad.' "

"This is deep," I say. "This is very deep."

"Tell me about it. She said that even though we were separated and we weren't sleeping together, she said she wanted me back."

"Under her terms."

"Yes."

"Or under the normal terms of marriage."

"But who is to say—one person's normal is another person's abnormal. I think it's abnormal for someone to enjoy sex but hold back their climax because they want control." He slaps the palm of his right hand with the back of his left hand.

"I think it's abnormal to vacillate from 'I love you, I love you' to 'I hate you.' " He slaps the palm of his left hand with the back of his right hand.

" 'I hate you. I want to have your baby.' " He throws both palms up, cocks his head, and shrugs. "She told the woman in the hotel room, 'He's not going to marry you. You're ugly.' "

"Do you think the two years of counseling is going to work?"

"I fluctuate between yes and I hope so. If I didn't want it to work, I'd just go to the counseling, wait out the two years, and, since we now have a prenuptial, mid-stream, I'd just file for the divorce.

"The agreement would hold up in a court of law. She could probably break it, arguing that I didn't act in good faith, but it would take her so much time and money to break it, and I could sit on the fence while she's spending all her money trying to do it, and I think she's too smart for that.

"I would like for it to work out, but I don't know. I would just have to see how it works out. For one thing, there is a problem, and though some people might not think it's a problem, it's a problem."

"What?"

"I just told you—sex. I like sex every night. Seven nights a week. I get tired of the no's. I get tired of the excuses, especially when I believe the excuses are a control mechanism, okay. Consciously or subconsciously they are a control mechanism because that's the way she is, okay.

"I don't have to have it every night. Nothing happens to me if I don't. It's like coffee. Some people like to wake up every morning with a cup of coffee, and their day is not right until they have that cup of coffee.

"Sex is a part of love, okay. And to me, I think that love is one of the most important ingredients to anybody who is successful, because you have to know about love in order to understand about bringing things together. It's very important. It's a missing part of me, ah, yeah!

"But since I've consolidated at a certain level by having this house, it becomes a trade-off. I have this missing part, but is that going to result in a bigger setback than giving up the house and starting all over, at my age?

"That's the way I feel now. I'll see in a year or two. Maybe the counseling will work. Maybe we'll get back together. It's not as tense as it was, and that helps.

"I could give it about two years the way it's going right now, because there are some things that I will have to reconsider at that point—one, not being in love, if that is the case; and two, not having children. I have a concern about that. Do you think the two years of counseling is going to work?" he asks, suddenly cocking his head to the side, smiling, looking for an answer, an opinion, making conversation, getting input.

"That's up to the two of you. You both have the control to make it work or not work."

"Depending on what?" he asks, smiles and narrows his gaze on me as if he is my branch manager, seeing how sharp I am. Or he may or may not be trying to see how transparent or nontransparent he is.

"Everybody's motives seem fairly obvious to me. I think you two both like the game."

"You think so? Why would you say that?" He intensifies his amused scrutiny.

"It's about adventures and opportunities," I say, leaving him to put whatever meaning he wants to my ambiguous remark.

"Yeah," he says. "And somebody is better than nobody."

"Precisely."

"I'm not going to be alone for a very long period of time because I do like female companionship. I like to laugh. I like to joke. I like to do-the-do."

"Then, that's your answer," I say.

He laughs.

THE "WE" THAT
Love CREATES

She had come back to her mother's house in a neighborhood that had changed a lot since she was born there in 1970. She said that since coming back home she had had a lot of time to think about what love had done to her. She had had time to ask herself a hundred times if there was something wrong with the way she loved. Back in 1970 this had been a neighborhood of rather substantial sand-colored brick row houses owned by stable black families. In the winter of 1995 Fullerton Street seemed sinister.

The houses were now rundown. Many of the houses were occupied by renters rather than owners. Some of them had been cut up into rooming houses.

She sat by a bay window, looking out at the street. I was on the sofa in back of her looking at her sleeping baby, a five-month-old caramel-colored girl with a jet-black helmet of curly hair.

"What is love?" I asked.

"There are several answers to that question, actually. One, there is the good, old-fashioned romantic Cinderella stuff, and yes, even after all that happened, I still believe in that crap. I told you I was a hopeless romantic. And second, there is all that physical garbage. And the third one would speak more of a spiritual kind of thing," she said without turning around.

There was no need for me to rush. Her mother and father were off at work. We had all day. "Which one of those accounts for the fact that you, from your middle-class background, could have ended up in the dead of winter pregnant and homeless, sleeping on park benches in Philadelphia?''

"Depends on the time of day," she laughed. "Or night," she laughed. "Or month or year," she laughed.

We didn't talk for a while. I wanted to wait to see how she wanted to enter the painful space that memory must have been for her. When I had asked her if she was willing to be interviewed, she had said, "Absolutely," in a very crisp way. There may have been some pride in her having survived what she had survived, but I wanted to wait to see.

"The first time I ever fell in love I was only fourteen years old. It was with a young man named Rasheed, from the next block, and we started going together when I was thirteen—going to dances together and holding hands and kissing in the movie.

"I don't know when I started loving him. I don't think it was intentional. I don't think I was mature enough to do anything intentional. It just happened.

"Rasheed had a sense of purpose. He had the promise of becoming a professional, and, therefore, he would be able to support a family and children. He would help me to live out the Cinderella promise of 'They lived happily ever after,' with me staying home and taking care of our very own house. I could see it."

"That must have been about 1984," I said, so that I could keep in mind how recent this had all been.

"Yes, about then. One night walking home from a movie we stopped off in the elementary school playground and started necking and got a little carried away and did the thing, which was unlike most women describe it. It was a truly wonderful experience.

"Love in that context made me feel whole and complete and beautiful despite what I really am," she said. In explanation she said: "I've never felt like an attractive woman. I always thought my two sisters were more attractive than I was.

"I look at pictures of myself and I realize that the woman in the pictures is drop-dead gorgeous, which I must have been at certain times in my life. I got an old issue of *Ebony,* and there is a picture of the movie star Dorothy Dandridge, and I look like I could have been her twin sister, except for the old hairdo that she had. But the beauty is only in the picture. Personally, I've always felt rather hideous.''

I noticed that there was a kind of pride in her choice of words, but no strain. This confirmed what everyone said about her. ''She's a very smart girl,'' they said. ''I don't understand it.'' ''She's brilliant, but she doesn't have what you would call common sense,'' someone said.

Her own impression of herself as hideous might have come from the fact that she had a very serious face that sometimes made her look older than she was.

''My mother always plastered the walls with pictures of both my older sisters. My oldest sister won all the beauty contests and everything, and she was a graceful swan.

''And my next older sister could open her mouth and the most beautiful sounds in the world would come out,'' she said as she walked away from the window to look at her sleeping baby.

I decided to help her with the story she was constructing. ''And then there was you.''

''Yes, and then there was me, who couldn't do anything except maybe fuck real good and make a couple of guys real happy. My partners were always very, very happy because I gave of myself, and for that moment in time I made them the center of the universe.

''I didn't play. I did some very serious fucking. I was very concerned about serving, about reaching his soul. That was my intention. Even at fourteen in the playground.''

''That's what love is to you?''

''In truth, every man I've ever loved has either abused me or abandoned me, one or the other. There's no question about there being a pattern, but I didn't think about that at first. All I thought about was that it felt good, and I made them feel good because I wanted to be loved.

"At that time I was literally trying to become one with my partner. Literally. I thought that was the way it was supposed to be done. What did I know? As a matter of fact, there were times when I literally did become one with my partner. Our coming together literally was very fluid, like melting bars of gold, we flowed together."

I put a cliché out there to see where she would go with it. "That's heavy," I said.

"No shit, Sherlock," she countered with another cliché, which seemed to prove that she flowed to whatever level the person talking to her was on.

"Even the first time it was like that?" I asked.

"The next morning Rasheed called me, broke up with me, and started going with another young lady."

As she spoke I kept thinking how when you're that young, you never think that you are that young. You don't think of yourself as a little girl, but this all happened when she was a little girl.

"The other young lady was only eleven. He was scared to death of getting me pregnant. He had plans for his life. He had a sense of what he was not going to do in order to get to doing what he wanted to do—be an engineer.

"We were basically young people from working-class families trapped in an old neighborhood of the city. Most of us were trying to get ourselves established so we could escape to the suburbs once we got out of college.

"I always fell in love with these guys who had big dreams. The next guy I fell in love with, Craig Miller, was in college and on his way to being a National Football League star, which he eventually did become.

"Craig used to come to our house for Thanksgivings and other short vacations instead of going home. And he and I also did a lot of hand-holding. After going together for about two years, we went to the movies one night and we got a little too passionate, and soon after that he dumped me.

"This was the same thing that happened before. And at the time I think that Craig was still considering the priesthood, to tell you the truth, if the football thing didn't work out.

"The pattern was that when it gets intense, I get left. I think it's because I give too much of myself, and that can be very scary to the other person. The idea that love and sex could be scary, the idea that I, by sharing myself with another being, wholly, without question, freely, would scare a man away—I guess I never caught on to that too well. Not well enough to try to change it.

"It was not that I was some little slut. Up until this time I had had only five sexual partners, and with each one of them it was the same."

"Did it ever occur to you that you might be doing something different than other girls, or young ladies, do?" I asked.

"How would I know? I was very sheltered. I went to all-girls Catholic schools all my life. Daddy gave us everything. Whatever you asked for you got and then you got more. No matter what you had done—good, bad, or indifferent. Daddy is probably the most unconditionally loving human being in the world.

"Mom, she's probably the most critical, dogmatic human being in the world, on the surface, but deep down inside I found that my mother could love more deeply than any human being in the world.

"My mother was a mother for the entire neighborhood. She took in foster children. She would do for you, but then she would use what she had done for you to make you do right, as she saw it. But she never ceased to love and to continue to do all the while she was criticizing.

"So you could say I came from a very loving family although

we did not appear to be. I cannot think of a day when Momma and Daddy didn't fight or hassle each other. There was constant bickering in the family, but there was never any doubt in my mind that they loved me.

"They were not affectionate, so it was not an outward display of love. They were very loving nonetheless. Then both of my two sisters got pregnant, and I knew how much this broke my mother's heart. The year I turned seventeen my mother tried to commit suicide, and that was related to my sister being pregnant and unmarried. I was the one who found my mother. And I knew how devastated she was, and so I vowed that I would be married before I was pregnant.

"After high school, I moved out of my mother's house because I couldn't stand being at home anymore. I was out on my own and I was dating a guy named Tyree, and I was also dating Roberto, the baby's father. They both came to my apartment the same night, and they were both determined to outwait each other.

"Tyree had a car and Roberto didn't, and public transportation stopped running at two A.M. So after two A.M. Roberto had to stay. Tyree left. I wanted a man to take care of me, and so when Roberto proposed to me I accepted. That's literally how it happened. He moved into my apartment.

"I got pregnant about a month after we got married, but he beat that one out of me. He literally beat three babies out of me. He once left me lying in a pool of my own blood in the elevator.

"He was on drugs at the time and I didn't know it. The only jobs he could get were pumping gas and custodial jobs and things, all of which he thought were beneath him. They truly were beneath him. After we got married he quit his job.

"I got caught up in his argument that the world was being mean to him and I should take care of him if I loved him. I wanted to love him and be loved by him, and so I vowed to take care of him.

"I realized now that he felt that people were to be used, and he justified the use of them by being very generous in little things that didn't matter much. I got caught up in wondering if he was doing this consciously or if he really did think of himself as a generous person.

"He was very, very charming until he would get tanked up. Then the true him would come through. He was Dr. Jekyll/Mr. Hyde. But I was willing to work. I worked at a college for a while and I worked as a policy typist. But we couldn't keep the rent paid because he drank up the little bit I made.

"I was still hoping to capture the Cinderella dream with the person with whom I had made the vow. He was a master at saying 'I'm sorry, baby,' and I got caught up in trying to show him that if he was sorry there were certain things he should do to prove it."

"What about him attracted you?" I asked.

"He was brilliant intellectually, though undereducated. He was a pretty boy. He was the dreamer. He had an IQ of about 162, I think it was," she said in a voice that let me know that she regarded IQ as an ultimate determiner of worth.

"I tried to love him. I think he loved me. I think he loved possessing me. In his eyes I was very pretty, and I had a body of death. It was pride of ownership. He did own me."

"What did he look like?"

"He was the prettiest man I ever saw in my whole life. God, he was pretty. He looked a lot like a masculine-looking Johnny Mathis—not a speck of fat to be found. God, he was pretty."

"And why, did you say, you stayed?"

"I had made a vow, hadn't I? Isn't that what a vow is—better or worse? So this was worse. I looked at his family and thought that he was going to improve."

I looked at her for a long time to let her know that the reasons she gave didn't seem to be enough to make me understand.

"I had made a vow and I take a vow seriously. And then there was this entity called 'the we.' It had a life of its own and I didn't want to kill it."

I wanted to talk with her about "the we," but I knew that I had better finish the interview first. I wanted to tell her that you have to be careful about losing "the me" in "the we." I knew this was a big issue for young women like her—having a life outside "the we."

I was thinking about the sociology of it: how a lot of middle-class black girls have identity problems in a society that pictures being black as something very different than they are.

I kept thinking of the song that asked how can you lose yourself to someone and never lose your way. Then there were two other songs: "Stand By Your Man" and "Love Will Keep Us Together."

I had a daughter about her age and I hoped that my daughter would never give up too much of "the me" in order to form a "we," but I also hoped that she never focused so much on "me" that she could never really merge into a "we."

I thought about the phrase "cosmic loneliness," which I came across in a book by Zora Neale Hurston. The only way to end cosmic loneliness is to form a "we," I thought. That's the dangerous part.

What could I say? I knew I didn't want to suggest the all-too-pervasive modern solution "Never give up yourself" because I felt that there was something beautiful about her ability to come out of herself, "and to share myself with another being, wholly, without questions, freely," as she described it.

"And so we got thrown out of eleven apartments in three years. And we would . . . and then we . . . and each time we . . ." I looked at her rather than listened to all these things that were happening to this "we" that slept on park benches and under bridges—this "we" that she didn't want to kill.

"I thought I could save the marriage. I was totally lacking in cynicism. I had a genuine belief in the goodness of all individuals. I accepted things at face value, as face value is perceived to be by the eye of the beholder.''

Finally I had to break in. ''A loss of self can make it possible for you to be led to bad places by the person you come out of yourself to be with. Then they have three selves—the you, the me, and the we—totally at their disposal. That's a nice position for him to be in.''

''No shit, Sherlock,'' she said. ''He had a keen sense of how unjust the system was when it came to dealing with black people. And he hated the pretense that the system was different and fair. Everything that he would read in the newspaper proved to him that he was right because he could give a different interpretation to everything that he read.

''I learned later that while he was in college he had been accused of date rape by a white girl and thrown out of college. He was about to be prosecuted when the girl said she had made the story up because she was angry with him because she was in love with him, but the girl's lawyer made his family sign an agreement that they would not sue before he would let the girl testify to his innocence.

''His parents were just happy that he wouldn't be going to jail, and so they signed the agreement for him. He was a minor then and they thought they would just send him to a black college down South, but he didn't want to go.

''He didn't believe in segregating himself racially. The girl was white, but he didn't dislike black or white people. In fact, one of the guys who used to stay at the apartment was this white guy who came from a fairly wealthy family who had been sexually abused by his stepfather.

''They would go to various black militant things to help protest against the system, but when his white friend was not accepted they would leave.

"He didn't even blame the girl's family because he said they weren't doing anything but protecting their money. He didn't blame his parents because they were afraid. He did blame the college for wanting to believe he was guilty before anything was proven, and he didn't trust that he could win in court against the college if he sued them for throwing him out—that was the system in America for a black man—'Guilty unless you can prove you're innocent,' he would say.

"This is 'the we' that you became a part of."

"I thought it was my obligation as a black person to accept this view of the system. He blamed the system. He didn't blame black women. If anything, he blamed his good looks, because when people used to compliment him for being good-looking he would say: 'Brothers better-looking than I am get thrown in jail, or get shot, every day.'

"He blamed the system. He could make long speeches about how the system could do anything it wanted to the individual because the system had the power and the individual was powerless. It all made sense to me, but being taken in by it wasn't the main reason. The main reason was I wanted to be loved. I just thought that if I loved, then that love would be returned to me.

"I was taken in by the fact that he had a very kind heart in public. He could, and would, charm the pants off of anyone. As soon as we were married he felt he didn't have to deal with the system anymore. As I said, he quit his job and began staying home. With nothing to do he began to drink, and soon began to use drugs.

"In order to get the drugs, because he didn't know the street scene, he had to begin hanging out with other marginal people. He began bringing them to the apartment, and when one of them didn't have a place to stay they would stay there, sleeping on the floor.

"But then we'd get thrown out and we'd be on the street, sometimes in the winter. We'd have blankets from the apartment they put us out of. At first I had a car. We started out in a parking lot in the car and then the car died. And it sat in the same place for so long that the city eventually towed it off.

"I got pregnant, and so I finally convinced him to get his mother to let us move into her house, but she hastened to tell him that I had parents and that I should go back to my parents to live.

"But I didn't have the intestinal fortitude to call my mother and tell her that this was my situation. And so I was out on the streets by myself until I got picked up by the police and taken to a homeless shelter. I went from there to the hospital to deliver my baby. The hospital called my parents, and that's how I came back home."

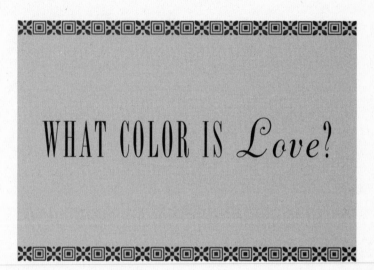

WHAT COLOR IS *Love?*

*T*wo nights before the wedding, when I interviewed Crystal Hollingsworth, the bride, she was as cheerful, carefree, and dreamy as she could be. One night before the wedding, when I interviewed Chris Chambers, the groom, he seemed tied in knots.

"It's natural for the prospective bride to be bubbling over and for the groom to be petrified," said the wedding adviser on the yacht they had rented for the wedding.

Two nights before, Crystal had said: "He's very good-looking. I'm not going to lie. I want some beautiful children. I'm not looking for Mr. Beautiful, but I do want some beautiful kids.

"He dresses well. That's a must. Smells good. Funny. He has a great sense of humor when you get to know him. I wouldn't marry him otherwise. I couldn't have someone who's serious twenty-four, seven, and stress me out.

"Everything that I ask I think I have to offer. I am considered a somewhat well-educated woman. I can discuss just about anything. I can sit there and watch the football games with him. I can discuss world affairs.

"I look good. I don't go around bragging about it, but I'm tall. I'm fit. I'm a dance instructor, remember. I dress well and expensive and I smell good, like I ask. I have a good sense of humor. I love having fun and I'm honest. And I don't want anybody who's going to cheat on me, because I don't do that. So I found the man of my dreams even though he was not the man I dreamed of.''

The night after I interviewed Crystal, I interviewed Chris. He said: ''I allowed myself to fall in love with Crystal. I allowed myself to fall in love every time I fell in love. No one has just captivated me to the degree that I just couldn't help myself. They were conscious decisions, each and every time.''

The day of the wedding the physical contrast between the two of them was quite remarkable. She seemed delighted, in a white wedding gown. He seemed tense, in his white tuxedo and red bow tie. He was thirty-seven years old. She was nineteen. She weighed about 125. He weighed more than 250.

Standing in front of the preacher, beside his black best man, you had to look at him twice before accepting that he was black. That's how light his skin was.

Looking at him and the preacher, who was white, if you didn't look at him twice you would probably not notice that he wasn't white. In contrast, Crystal was the color of dark, rich coffee.

The boat pulled away from the pier at seven P.M. The wedding ceremony was first. The schedule was designed to get them married first so that the rest of the cruise could be devoted to celebration.

A short, plump woman who looked like she might be part African American and part European American was about to sing the wedding solo. She had bright, smiling eyes under droopy eyelids.

She sang that he should love his wife like nobody has loved her come rain or come shine.

Crystal and Chris stood looking deeply into each other's eyes as the boat rocked on the waves with the soloist reminding them that some days might be cloudy and some might be sunny, that they might be in or out of money; but love had to remain.

Two nights before the wedding, Crystal had said: "It's funny how your dreams of love and marriage can come true, exactly as you want them to, and yet they don't look anything like you thought your dream would look. I had very definite ideas about love and marriage.

"I knew what I wanted and didn't want, but I had never pictured what the guy would look like. I could have never pictured getting married to a man like Chris. The only part that fits the picture is the boat. I always wanted to get married on a boat," she had said.

"And this desire to be married on a boat increased when I got to Miami, where a lot of people get married on boats. I came down here not looking for a husband. I came down to attend the University of Miami to study languages.

"I wanted to be a language teacher or a dance teacher. I had studied dance all my life in Hartford, Connecticut. That's where I came from. I loved it down here so I stayed down here during the summers, because summer is the best time of year here.

"I just loved being on the beach all day. And then I taught dance at night, and two days a week I taught English as a second language courses. That's where I met Chris. I was his daughter's dance instructor. You know, he has a fourteen-year-old daughter and a twelve-year-old son."

One day before the wedding Chris had said: "My mother is white, but I definitely consider myself to be a black man. Not consider myself to be, I am a black man. I was raised in a black neighborhood in Detroit.

"In fact, my mother was the only white person in the neighborhood. She wanted me and my brother to be raised around black people because she didn't want us to encounter the prejudice that we might have come up against if she had taken us to a white neighborhood.

"But contrary to that, I think it was harder for her to fit into a black neighborhood than it would have been for us to fit into a white neighborhood. I just think the truth was that she liked being around black people.

"When she was very young, sixteen, she had got pregnant with me by a black policeman who was married. He stayed married and my mother loved him so much that she stayed with him for years, as his outside woman.

"She got pregnant with me and then she got pregnant with my younger brother, Roger. I saw my father quite often because he could come by whenever he was on duty, on patrol. He would stop by and he and my mother would get high on coke and they would stay in the bedroom. Sometimes he would stay the night. My mother loved him very much and me and my brother liked him. What did we know?

"The money was always there. He must have been doing something other than straight up-and-up police work at the time because he gave my mother enough money to live on. No one in the neighborhood knew that he had another family by a black woman out in Southfield. I didn't find out until I was a teenager. I just thought he was gone from home a lot.

"My father and mother loved that ghetto life. I didn't love it, I just thought I was tied to it because I was very proud to be black. I was a big kid, even then, and I was a fighter, and I made it be known that I would fight if anyone tried to say I wasn't black."

In my interview with Crystal, she had said: "I knew that love was very rare. I thought I was going to have to wait for it, but I was willing to wait. I was young. I knew the person had to be right, but I had no idea who the right person would be. If you had told me it would be Chris, I would have laughed.

"But it's funny how he filled the bill for so many of the things I knew I had to have in a husband. Chris has a very generous personality.

"I mean, you see him and you see this tough guy, but you would be surprised. Ask his daughter. They just love each other. He's harder on his son because he wants his son to be tough, but as far as a woman is concerned he's a pushover. He's extremely generous.

"I think a lot of people in America are very selfish. One thing I noticed when I started studying languages, when you study the English language, I never understood why, whenever you're talking about yourself, *I* is capitalized.

"You know, there's so much emphasis on the self. It's 'I this,' 'I that,' 'I the other.' I have studied five languages and in none of them is the word for *I* capitalized. It's not. A lot of people are only out for themselves. Chris is different. That's probably why I love him most."

On the yacht, the wedding ceremony was coming to a close. Standing in front of the preacher, Chris said his part of the wedding vows: "Today we cross an invisible line."

Crystal said: "We leave behind our yesterdays and start our lives anew."

Chris said: "The past is over. We will concern ourselves only with the future."

Crystal said: "It's a new day, a new commitment, a new life." She started to cry.

For a moment it seemed that Chris might cry too. His eyes

filled up with water. "The vows we take today will change us forever."

Crystal put a lot of emphasis in the next line: "I take them gladly."

Chris said: "I take them gladly too."

Crystal said: "Chris Chambers, I promise to love you, to protect you, and to be faithful to you for all the days of my life."

Chris said: "Crystal Hollingsworth, I promise to love you, honor you, and always be honest with you. I will be faithful to you for all the days of my life."

The day before Chris had said: "Crystal has never been in love. We both took that into consideration. I didn't want to rush things, but after a while she was more eager than I was.

"Having Crystal to love is very important. It's very difficult for people to focus and to concentrate. Me being a businessperson, I don't have time to be chasing love in all the wrong places, so to speak, so I had made up my mind to do without a woman and just concentrate on making my business a success and raising my two children.

"I have been very serious since I was about sixteen. I knew what I wanted. I set goals. I grew up in the 'hood, if you will. I experienced that lifestyle, the fast life, as they call it. I didn't want that."

"Had you ever been in love before?" I asked.

"Yes, I was married before, and I would never have gotten married if I had not been in love. I was in love with my children's mother, but before that I was in love in high school. And this will show you how I've always tried to be serious about life.

"The first woman I was in love with, she made straight A's, she came from a good family background. She seemed to be very level-headed. She cooked. I don't want to be sexist, but men are attracted by that, and she was attractive.

"She was slender, all those kinds of things. I guess it was out of the ordinary, being a light-complexioned guy, I used to have this thing about long-haired, red-bone women, right. This woman was very light-complexioned.

"Yet I was always curious about the dark-skinned ones, but hanging out with the guys, and so forth, I was color struck. I was a typical black man. I had that slave mind-set. Black men have been conditioned since way back when that if a woman is dark, she's more like the field slave. You don't want her. You want the more prestigious, closer-to-being white one.

"I didn't realize what I was doing, but in that sense, that's what it was, and so I wanted to date the kind of woman who would make the fellas say that Chris had a fine woman.

"However, my personal belief, from mere observation and interaction, men have a better chance of getting along with a dark-skinned woman. She's less concerned about 'You serve me.' I think that's a historical thing that happened. If a sister was light-skinned, it's a stereotype to a degree, but for the most part it seems to be fairly true in generalities, she's used to being served. She just thinks she's fine and she's God's gift to men.

"Not all of them. Some dark-skinned women, I wouldn't take 'em with a shovel. If they were giving a new car away with her I wouldn't take her.

"But in general, I just think dark-skinned women are less likely to be hung up on how they look, as opposed to what's in their heads and getting along with their men. I feel in particular that the brothers have chased light-skinned women for so long, she's got fifty million guys chasing after her and so she's less inclined to appreciate the qualities that a good black man might bring to the table.

"Darker-skinned women are just more apt to appreciate an

intelligent, sincere black man when he comes along and says, 'Hello, how are you?'

"Well, this girl in high school that I was in love with would be considered—quote unquote—pretty. But at the same time her dad was a real protective dad. They wouldn't let her go out and date.

"I had to go over to her house and see her under parental supervision. She was actually even a virgin at the time. She was fourteen. I was sixteen. I was very serious. I knew what I wanted in the relationship.

"Later she changed on me. She turned sixteen and her mother and father said, 'You can go out now.' Before, I was the only person she could see. I could have seen other people. I was a football star. I had a car, but many Friday nights I put off other things to go over there to be with her.

"I thought the favor would be returned in kind when she got old enough to date. But the moment she turned sixteen, she got buck-wild, basically. I had brought her a promise ring, as young men do. She had asked me for the ring. I was working as a caddie in the summer, carrying golf bags out in the hot sun, working like a slave, but I did it.

"I took my last paycheck because I was getting ready to go back into football practice in the fall, and so I gave her her ring. It was about a hundred dollars. You know, for a guy going to high school back in the eighties, that was a lot of money for a high school kid.

"I gave her her ring and within a week she completely changed on me. She tossed me to the curb, so to speak. There was a showdown at the arena that all the guys were going to take their girls to, and she told me she was going with someone else. I said, 'No problem.'

"I was into football anyway. I asked her was it one of her girlfriends, and she said no, or is it a cousin then, and she said no.

I began to get a little bit concerned, so finally I asked, 'Is it a guy?' and she said, 'Yes.'

"I started laughing because I thought she was yanking my chain. I mean, I wasn't a chump, you know what I mean. I was a man's man, if you will, and so when she finally told me this, you know, I couldn't believe it, but she was serious. And so to me it was very heartless, very compassionless, and I felt it was completely out of left field, out of the dark.

"Frankly and ultimately we had engaged in sex before she turned sixteen, and in hindsight it was probably a little bit too early for her to have done that. I don't know if that had something to do with it or not.

"I don't know. Maybe she felt like if I was her only experience she was missing something. I've never had any complaints about sexual performance along the way. She dated a few other men, but she ultimately married the man she played on me with. In fact, they are married today. I don't know. He was wearing a Jheri Curl when Jheri Curls were out of style.

"He was dark-skinned, she was light-skinned. I have had very few light-skinned women really attracted to me. Me, as a light-skinned male, had more of a difficult time attracting light-skinned women. This might not be true across the board, but it was true for me."

On the boat the dinner was buffet-style, and there were tables in the dining room and some tables on both the forward and aft decks where people could take their full plates. Uniformed waiters and waitresses served beverages as land and sunlight receded behind us.

"Were you afraid marrying a man with a daughter only five years younger than you?" I had asked Crystal before. "I've heard of women marrying men with daughters older than they are, but you, you're not a fancy stepper. You're regular folk.''

"*Afraid* wouldn't be the right word. My first concern was there were a lot of things that I wanted to do with myself before I could be with someone else and make that person completely happy. I have a little bit of growing up to do still. Spiritually I'm not where I want to be. I'm not one of those people who talk about God here and there, but I do believe there is a higher power, a certain way you should live your life, and I don't think I can do that even yet. I have made some progress, but I'm not to the point where I can be comfortable to say I can live my life totally as I should. I want someone like his daughter to look at me and say: 'I want to be just like her when I grow up.' In order to do that I got to grow up some more myself.

"I was pretty spoiled when I was growing up. I'm so used to having everything that I ever wanted. For example, I don't know how to save. I can just go somewhere and see a suit and I can spend my whole paycheck on it.

"Sometimes I can be bluntly honest with people and sometimes I hurt people's feelings. I'm never going to lie, but I want to be able to work around their feelings so I can know how to say things in a way that is not so blunt.

"I have to work on being more patient. I want what I want when I want it. That's what people who know me would say. I have to work on that.

"I go to church and I talk to people. There are a couple of women at church in my life that I admire. I wanted to stick around and observe a lot. I did consider myself a baby in many ways, but all the men here in Miami seemed so much more immature.

"The men I was meeting had a long way to go. The way they approach you. A guy might say, 'Don't I know you from somewhere? You're a model?' I say to myself that that's so immature, 'You can't do better than that? Come on.' Another one might say,

'Where did you go to school? I swear I know you.' I say, 'Jesus, help me here.' They were so immature.

"I didn't even date in Miami. I was waiting for a man to make an honest approach, like 'I been looking at you and I just wanted to come by and talk to you and see what's up.' To be plain honest, 'I think you look good.' If he saw me laughing he could say, 'You seem nice. I would like to know your name.' Whatever is real to that person, but coming to me and saying I think I saw you on the cover of a magazine, come on, you know, I was hearing those lines all the time.

"They kill me, the lines that come out. I think I heard them all. The worst one I got was when I had on a short little top and some shorts and this guy said, 'Stand up so I can look at you.' I said: 'Excuse me.' I had never met the man before in my life and he came over and said, 'Stand up so I can check you out.' Am I a piece of merchandise? What is wrong with them? Not even 'Hi, what's your name?' Just, 'Stand up so I can look at you.'

"So I had turned off to all approaches. No matter what, I just automatically turned off. I wouldn't even consider it. But the thing about Chris is that he never approached me.

"He would bring his daughter to dance class, but unlike the other parents who would go to get coffee or go run errands while their child was in class, he would always stay, and I was never nervous in front of him.

"In fact, I noticed that I liked dancing and teaching with him watching, but I didn't think there was anything to it. I just thought he was one of those parents who wanted to make sure his daughter was getting her, or his, money's worth.

"He never said anything, but then one time I went to talk to him and his daughter about enrolling her in the next class, and his daughter said, 'My daddy likes you.'

"He was so embarrassed. I saw this great big man get so embarrassed. It was almost like he wanted to turn and run. This huge man who I knew had been a pro football player. And his daughter didn't help him. She was always the talkative one, but she didn't say anything. She just stood there like the two of us had trapped him.

"I think that's when my heart went out to him. I learned later that he had never told his daughter that he liked me. She did that all on her own because she knew him."

On the boat the disk jockey played a variety of music, and people danced under the moonlight on the aft deck, where the wedding ceremony had been held. Dancing on a boat was a lot of fun because some steps were intentional and some had to be taken to keep balanced. Doing that and staying in rhythm added an extra challenge.

Everyone seemed to be having a great time. I got to meet all four of the parents, and they all seemed quite happy about the wedding. Chris's daughter tried to show the old folks how to do the macarena.

The night before, when Chris and I had talked about his daughter, he had said that she was like her mother. She had a good heart but he was afraid for her because of the way she was raised.

"A lot of the kids now who grew up, their fathers are doctors, well-established lawyers, businesspeople like me, what have you, want to get into the ghetto lifestyle. The danger has a tendency of attracting them and whatnot.

"That bothers me more so about my daughter than my son. He's more like me. He's methodical. Nothing is going to pull him out of his direction. But my daughter is very easy to influence, like her mother."

"Did you meet her mother in Detroit?" I asked.

"No. I met her in Miami. After my first love, I dated other girls during high school, but I didn't let myself fall in love. I went out with a lot of girls. They were all light-skinned. I was a football star, a big man in school, so to speak. I didn't have my choice of women, but I could do okay.

"Physical appearance has been, historically, the first thing that most men care about. I mean, it's always been beauty and sex for security. Basically, men wanted an attractive woman who looked like a goddess. She didn't have to be smart. She didn't have to do a whole lot of things.

"If she was beautiful, he didn't care how she was as long as she gave him sex, and basically, women wanted a man that was wealthy. Very few women will turn down a millionaire. Women knew I could make a lot of money playing football, so I had women.

"And basically I chose to come and play at the University of Miami because I knew it was either Miami or Southern California or UCLA. I wanted to be in a place where I could get the kind of acceptance that I didn't get with black people or with white people deep down. Deep down I had some color confusion.

"So I came to Miami thinking I was going to find this woman who was going to be a quarter Indian, a quarter Hispanic, a quarter African-American, and a quarter Brazilian, or whatever. Nobody knew what the hell she was.

"I didn't have the color problem. Women had a problem with me, let's put it that way. I can feel myself as a black man or a white man, very much so, and the black man in me is very much interested in the light-skinned woman, but the white man in me is very curious about the darker ones. I think here again the black man has been duped—while he is pursuing the light-skinned woman, the white man is really fascinated by the darker one.

"In college, for the first time, I dated white women. I heard the hype and I wanted to find out what everybody was talking about, what was I missing? They were cool, but I had no reason to go outside of my race, straight up.

"Then I fell in love with my children's mother. She was light-skinned. Again, I was getting close to this dark-skinned girl. On campus I was always careful to dress in a certain way, very neatly, sometimes suits and ties a lot, because I didn't want people thinking of me as a jock, an athlete with nothing else to offer. I was cool. I wasn't a nerd, but people may have perceived me as being a big nerd, which I preferred to being perceived as a football player. I wore glasses and I guess I looked like a nerd.

"I was talking to this dark-skinned girl and she was friendly, but she wouldn't go out with me. I don't know what she thought I was.

"At the same time my children's mother was noticing me. She thought that I was a nerd. She told me this later, and I asked her, 'Why would you want to date a nerd?' I guess my opinion is the answer is, nerds make money.

"She came up to me and asked me if I would like to go out sometime. This was a pleasant surprise for me actually. I was tired of always having to chase women and face being rejected, because I did think of this dark-skinned girl's actions as a rejection.

"I felt like a volleyball or something, so my children's mother stepped to me, and that was fine, so we started dating. It wasn't love.

"In fact, there was someone back home that she was dating. At the same time we had an agreement. I was very straight up and direct with her. Our agreement was that whenever she was back home she could date this guy; and when she was on campus, I was the only person she would date. How realistic or silly that was in hindsight I would not venture to say, but it worked fairly well.

"What happened was this girl became attracted to me more so than I actually intended for her to. She started buying me stuff despite my telling her not to; because I'm not a user of women. I don't feel comfortable with women giving me gifts.

"I think it makes a man slouchy when he's always expecting

gifts from his woman, and whatnot. Call it sexist, but I want to be able to be the breadwinner for my mate. That's just because I think it's the right thing to do.

"I was fascinated with her tenacity. She was relentless. She didn't give up. She seemed to be very sweet, very nice. Always bringing me things, bringing me food after football practice.

"She was a fascinating young lady and she seemed to have a good heart. Frankly, I wanted someone who had been hurt before so they would know what hurt felt like so they wouldn't be as apt to hurt me. Frankly, I vowed that after I got hurt the first time, if I got hurt again somebody might get hurt for real. And I made that point up front. That's just how I am. I'm just straight up.

"So she quit this guy back home and I felt somewhat obligated. I just gave in. That was fourteen years ago. I haven't been in love since then. I was playing pro football and traveling a lot.

"My wife and daughter stayed with my mother in Michigan. We then had a son. I had bought my mom a better house not far from where we grew up. She didn't want to leave the ghetto. She liked that lifestyle. My dad and my mother were still going together and there were drugs around the house and my wife got into a drug thing and she got into the fast life.

"I didn't know the extent until I was injured and had to end my football career after four years. I came home and wanted to get my kids out of that lifestyle. I had some good connections here in Miami, so I came down here expecting my wife to follow.

"She took off to New York and then I went to New York and literally kidnapped my children. I was afraid I was going to hurt somebody, and the only reason I didn't was because I knew I couldn't afford to go to jail. I had made up my mind that I was going to raise my kids by myself, because I didn't have trust in anybody else to do it."

* * *

On the boat I got a chance to talk with Chris's dad. He had a detective's manner about him. He asked questions and then he seemed to pause in order to weigh the answers. Chris's mother seemed very happy to have this uninterrupted time with him. They seemed happy with each other.

Crystal's mom and dad were legally separated and so they didn't spend a lot of time together. Each moved about the boat getting acquainted with other guests. Crystal made sure that I got a chance to talk to her mom. She put her face next to her mom's. "We look like sisters, huh?"

Her mother said: "I'm not your sister. She's always tried to pretend that she's my sister so she wouldn't have me telling her what to do," her mom said to me.

The night I interviewed Crystal I had asked her: "What is love?"

"There could be a lot of answers to that," she had said. There are so many aspects to love. There could be the physical, you have the spiritual, you have the mental. I am completely in love with Chris.

"The mental part means that we can talk. The spiritual part means that we have the kind of hookup where you don't have to talk to be connected. The physical part means passion. We have not had sex. I'm not a virgin, but he and I decided not to have sex together until the wedding night. I'm his virgin.

"He's in good shape and so he has a lot of energy. But for me it's not only the physical act. It's just the touching in there, you know, the holding, kissing, in there, just all of that. And the words. We've had that. He says that I am delicious to his eyes. He says I'm like French roast coffee."

"One spoon of sugar or two?"

"Four."

"Okay."

"He says that I am cute. I can be very cute when I put on my baby's voice. When I call him Daddy, which, since I know he's not my daddy, it's all right. It's just a form of play that I do when he tries to be mean.

"He says that I am adorable when I dance for him."

THE MORE *Love*

CHANGES

I'm still like I was twenty years ago," Billy said. "I'm still afraid of love, although I wouldn't use the word *afraid* now. Is that the word I used when you talked to me back then?"

I read from the story I had written on him in *Love, Black Love* back in 1978.

I skipped around, reading portions that I had underlined in preparation for this interview: " 'I was in love once. Yeah, I can say I was in love one time, when I was nineteen,' " I read. "That's you?"

"That's me."

I continued to read: " 'That's all I needed. One time. I was in love with a nice girl, man. Beautiful, sensitive, affectionate, all that. So I can't complain about that part. She was great. I loved her and I'm sure she loved me, but I broke it up, intentionally.' "

I asked: "You ever think much about her?"

"No, not really. There have been other women since then that I loved that erased that memory."

"But they say the first love is the best."

"In a way it is, but memory fades. I used to think about her a lot, but now if you asked me I could name four women that I loved since then just as much. One of them I married for a short time and we tried to love each other as man and wife. We struggled at it, but I don't like emotional struggling."

"Too painful?"

"Too confusing. It gets in the way."

"That's what you said back then. You said it interfered with your pursuit of your dream, or something like that. Did you achieve your dream?"

"In a way."

"You're rich. That's what you said you wanted to be, rich."

"I'm not rich, but I've had a rich life, which I wouldn't have had if I had stayed in love with that girl."

"But you said you wanted to be rich."

"Okay, so I am rich. I don't have any more money than I had then, but I'm rich because I learned how to accept myself for who I am. That's wealth."

"Accept the fact that you are afraid of love."

"Like I said, I wouldn't use the term *afraid* right now, or we could use that term. When it looks like things are getting too ugly or too good, getting too sweet, I do back away so I can get control of my emotions. That's why I fuck around with this stuff." He took a marijuana joint out of his pocket and lit it, drew some smoke into his lungs, held it, and then let it out. He repeated this before he offered the joint to me.

"No, I don't mess," I said.

"I do it to control my emotions during good times more than I do bad times. I think I have a limited capacity for happiness," he said.

I read some more from the 1978 interview. " 'I messed with her head every chance I got, because I wanted to break it up. No, I can't say I did it intentionally, but when I think back on it, I knew I must have had this subconscious desire to get her away from me. Thinking back on it, what I realize is that I was, and still am, afraid of love.' " I stopped reading.

He had been listening intently.

I asked: "What word would you use now?"

"I don't know. I don't know. It's very strange. See, the truth is that I've been in love, sweet love, many times since then, but . . ."

I cut him off and began reading again: " 'I love. I love fried chicken. . . . No. I love watermelon.' "

"Is that what I said?" He seemed quite pleased with himself for having said that.

"That's what you said. So, would you accept the idea that the more things change, the more they remain the same?"

"I still love chicken, but I haven't had all that much watermelon lately, but yeah, pretty much. Except I'm happier now than I was then."

"Happier being afraid of love?"

"Happier because I accept who I am. Happier because I've had enough freedom from struggling with love to make myself happy. You know, most people spend most of their lives struggling with love, or angry because they can't make the picture they have of love fit in with who they are."

"You look happy. How old are you?"

"I'm fifty-two."

"Yeah, you look like you're only forty."

"That's because I haven't been worrying about being in love."

"Statistics say that married men are happier and live longer than single men."

"That's because most single men spend their time looking for love. I don't."

"What do you do?"

"Love comes looking for me. I'm a good-looking guy. That's not ego-tripping and it's not even what I think because I don't think about it. It's what the behavior of women toward me tells me about myself," he said, and took the copy of *Love, Black Love* that I had been reading from. He scanned it as he spoke. He smiled.

"Women are very attracted to me. I didn't want to accept that back here," he said, pushing the book toward me for a moment before drawing it back to scan it again.

"It would have meant to me that I was conceited, and I'm not. It's only conceited if my saying that meant I was a snob or I was arrogant, egotistical, or vain, which, as you can see, I am not."

"No, you don't seem to be any of those things," I said. He didn't. And he was a good-looking guy.

"This is deep," he said, referring to something that he was reading about himself twenty years ago. "This is deep. 'I loved her too much. Thinking about the power she had over me gave me some scary, uncomfortable feelings,' " he read aloud after taking another long drag on his joint.

"Did each one of the women you've loved since then scare you in the same way?"

"Not exactly. I'd rather approach it from the positive side. Each one of the women excited me in a unique way, and I wouldn't have been free to enjoy the variety of excitement if I had been stuck with one woman, no matter how much I loved her at first."

"Yeah, okay."

He started reading again. " 'I wanted things other than her love, and the message I was getting from myself at the time is that when I was with her all I wanted was to be with her.' I would change that to say, 'I wanted things other than love itself.' That's how I matured." He took another drag. His eyes were getting glossy. He did seem a happy person.

"You weren't running from her love. You were running from love."

"I wasn't running from love. I was running from a specific embodiment that after a while would have represented something other than love. I was running toward love."

"And every time you get close you take another drag on your

joint and get on your horse and ride away looking for the abstraction—love.''

''Okay. That's true about me.''

''What about the women? Do you think it's fair to them?''

''Most of the women I loved, and the woman I was married to for a short while, most of them are friends. I talk to most of them from time to time. I think they are all happy that they once knew me.''

''And what about the first one, the one you loved so deeply at nineteen.''

''I wouldn't know where to find her, but I think she would be bitter. Not at me, although she would say it was me. She is really bitter, I hear, about what she did with her life, which is what she would have done with her life, most likely, if I had stayed with her. And she would have tried to do this with mine. So I would have had to leave her anyway.''

''Do you feel like you're cheating the 'supposed to be'?''

''That's the art of life. There is a general standard so-called 'supposed to be,' and I think you find happiness to the exact extent that you find out how you, individually, are supposed to not be.''

''As long as you don't hurt anyone?''

''Yeah, I try to be very careful about that.'' He found another one of the portions I had underlined and read it aloud: '' 'A lady can have fun with me. Enjoy me, but don't try to get too close. It bothers me. I just accept that about myself. I like to play the field; different women have different attractions.' This is deep. This is too deep.'' He laughed.

''You felt then as you feel now?''

''Pretty much. I was on my way then to feeling it. I was verbalizing it, but I wasn't necessarily living it fully. I had to go on a journey of self-discovery first.''

''Therapy?''

"I don't believe in therapy. All that therapy does is open up all your old wounds and help you grow a scab over them."

"So, what did your self-discovery entail?"

"I began reading a lot of books, like *The Superbeings; Mystics, Magicians, and Medicine People; The Celestine Prophecy; The Seven Spiritual Laws of Success*."

"That's very different from the stuff that you were reading twenty years ago. I took the book from him and found a place that I had not underlined. I read it. " 'I do read all those books about money, though: *The Rich and the Super-Rich; David Rockefeller; Supermoney*. If I take a book away with me on a weekend, it will be a book like that.' "

"I gave up wanting to be rich. I went to this psychic once and she said that I would have a hard time adjusting to being rich anyway. Some people are not meant to be rich. People might look at that as a flaw in character, but it's not. It's just a fact. In fact, the psychic said I would have a hard time dealing with the kinds of people I would attract if I was rich, especially the women. I could understand what she meant."

"Yeah, you would have attracted too many of them, and even your marijuana wouldn't have prevented the overload."

"And I would have had to use something stronger—cocaine."

"Or heroin," I suggested ominously.

"Or crack, who knows. I don't think heroin, or therapy, a life in therapy."

"Okay."

"Most people think that it is a terrible admission, in America, to admit that you, personally, are better off if you are not rich in material wealth. I think this happens to a lot of people. Say they have a talent which makes them a lot of money, but this talent might be just a love and ability with basketball, or a love and ability to sing, or act, or fuck with computers.

"They make a lot of money and the things that money can buy

brings a lot of things into their lives that were not meant to be there.''

"Like it would have brought a lot of women into your life who would not naturally have been there."

"Precisely, precisely. I would have never enjoyed the real nature of any woman. No one lets a rich man know the real truth about themselves. They even become something false and fantasized for the benefit of a rich man."

"But you like living in a sort of fantasy."

"That's the problem. I would have had too much of it, and it would have been outside the bounds of what I can control."

"I got you."

"This psychic told me a lot of good stuff, and I would have believed none of it unless it rang true to my experience, and it did. She said I was in love with love. She said that on the one hand I was timid, but on the other I had the desire to express my deepest feelings.

"She said that I was strong and I could either use that strength to face into life or use it to have the fortitude to pull back, pick-and-choose, and get involved in a lot of different things.

"She said that if I ever came to trust anyone, I would virtually become their slave."

"Damn! So women see that and they are attracted to it. They rush in and you pull away."

"Yup!"

"Wouldn't it be good to go all the way with it instead of playing with it?"

"In the world as it is, that is a truth about me that anyone would be tempted to misuse and abuse."

"So you're a person who doesn't give yourself totally because you have this tremendous capacity to give yourself totally."

"And the world's not ripe for that."

"Okay. Do you think it ever was?"

"I don't know, but everything is about power now. Who has power over who?"

"What else did this psychic say?"

"I went to the psychic over a period of six or seven months so I didn't have to go into therapy, where I would relive all the pain that this trait had caused me, and scab it over so I could get into what the therapist would call a healthy relationship—two people who have semihypnotized themselves so they can get into a 'mature, committed relationship.'

"Therapists work for society. They work to perpetuate a picture of how society should be according to some preconceived notion that they learned in school studying Freud, who wasn't all that much in love himself, according to what I read about him."

"What else did the psychic say about you and love?"

"She said a lot of stuff that helped with the journey. This is very, very consistent," he said, looking at something else I had underlined in the book. "It says here, 'I think I could marry a woman I didn't love. I think I would rather marry a woman I like rather than one I loved.' That's exactly what I did. This is amazing, except that didn't work. Why marry? Society says you should get married. That we have to have a certain number of marriages to carry on the race. That's why many people get married. It's their social duty, and then they go to therapists who help them put up with it."

He read the book for a while longer. "This is amazing. This is exactly what the psychic told me I was like without ever having met me before. I operate exactly like this except I do it on a more self-aware level."

"With regards to love, what one thing do you think you're now aware of that you were only subconsciously aware of then?"

He answered instantly, as if he kept the answer present in his mind at all times: "I like anticipation more than I love actualization."

"Now, that's deep."

"It's true."

"It's true as far as feelings are concerned, but what about sex? Do you like anticipating that more than you like making love?"

"The truth is that I'm not strictly about sex, which is also a brave admission for a black man, since that is what we're supposed to be all about. I don't know if that's in this interview because I may not have admitted it then. That's a hard thing for a black man to admit since we've all convinced ourselves that we are so sexually driven—you know, the old superstud thing."

"Superrich, superstud, superbeing?"

"I just like meeting women. I mean, that is intrigue. There is 'Will we end up in bed or will we not?' If we don't, I'm still happy, which is what's beautiful when you accept the fact that anticipation is just as exciting, or more exciting, than actualization.

"For example, I'm very excited about this woman I started going out with this summer. We've had four dates and I'm in love. She's in love.

"I met her in this restaurant where I was having lunch. This is what I mean by not chasing women. This woman had other choices, but she decided to sit at the table next to mine.

"A lot of guys were looking at her because she was very attractive. Little yellow Bermuda shorts, nice legs, had her hair in braids and all, but she gave me this big smile when she sat down. And there were guys in the restaurant who were—quote unquote—better-looking than I think that I am. This is why I say I'm not conceited."

"She may have detected that tendency in you to become a love slave. She might have said: 'This boy has potential.'"

"Okay."

"You don't trade on that look, do you?"

"No. I just look like what I look like. Anyway, when my entrée came she said, 'You're going to get fat,' in a kind of flip way. I said something to her and smiled to let her know that I was open. Now, whether this lady was interested in me or not, I could enjoy the fact that I felt she was—anticipation.

"Then she said, 'They have good food here.' I smiled and said something else, an extended bit of conversation so she didn't have to do all the work. I asked her to try some of the fish I had ordered. She took a forkful. 'Umm-m-m, that *is* good,' she said. I wasn't sure if I should make the next remark or not, but I decided to find out if she was just being friendly or if she was really interested, or just how interested she was, because I only wanted to talk with her if she was really interested."

"Because you can't handle rejection or disappointment," I said, just to mess with him a little.

"Okay, suppose that's true. Then what? Does that make me a bad person?"

"No. I just wanted to let you know that that's what it could mean."

"It does mean that, but it's perfectly all right. But it also means that I don't waste my time with someone who isn't interested in me, or only has a ho-hum interest, or is a ho-hum person, or our chemistry is ho-hum. Anyway, I waited, and finally she said: 'Do you know what time it is?' She was determined to pick me up.

"I said, 'No, but if you have to be somewhere at noon, you're late.' Then I started talking. 'How far do you have to go? Are you from around here? What do you do?' I told her some about myself and she was very lively, and so I steered the conversation toward a reason to ask her for her phone number.

"She wrote it down and said she really had to leave. I liked her from the first. She was very upbeat. Now, there are a lot of things I like to do in the city, places I like to go, so I called her up and we didn't talk much. I just invited her out to dinner.

"She was on her best behavior. I was on my best behavior. She was wearing this beautiful little outfit with a short skirt and a collarless matching blouse. I had on a silk shirt and silk-and-linen–blend trousers.

"We enjoyed each other. She was somewhat self-centered. I could tell that she liked a lot of attention being paid to her. I felt she deserved it. It was easy to do. There were so many things that you could give her honest compliments on—her spirit, her personality, her clothes, her outlook.

"Like I said: different women have different attributes. There are some who are not sure of themselves, and I do my best to make them appreciate themselves more, but this lady seemed to have a full appreciation of all that she was.

"I have this game I play with ladies. They seem to enjoy it. I ask them, if they could be anything they wanted to be, what would they want to be. And then sometimes I can get them to act like that during dinner, or in the bedroom—queen, princess, witch, singer, bird, movie star—whatever.

"She immediately said that she was all that she ever wanted to be. Okay, okay. Then she told me, 'And you are all that you ever want to be, really,' she said. That was the kind of remark that we let lie until later.

"She was a take-charge lady, but she was smooth with it. I wouldn't call her aggressive. I wouldn't say she came on strong. She was just very sure of herself, and so after a while we became very sure of each other.

"Now, a lot of people think that the prize in all of this is ending up in bed. The real prize is finding the exact moment to say: 'I got work in the morning. I know you do too. Maybe we'd better call it a night.'

"That's what I mean, anticipation can be better than actualization, and then it's not even anticipation. We're not teasing each other. We're waiting to see if it will happen naturally.

"I've been out with her four times. Each time it's been great. Meanwhile, I have this lady with this powerful, stressful job. She and I have had a sexual thing for about four years. She might date guys who are in the same power circles, but she's not necessarily going to bed with them, or she may be. I don't know.

"I do know that she likes to wind down with me and I like to make love to her. She might call me or I might call her and say: 'What're you doing?' and she starts talking and she might say: 'You want to come over' or I might say, 'Why don't you come over?'

"Everybody knows the deal. Does she love me? Yes. Do I love her? Yes. Do I love this new woman, or any new woman I've met since I've known her. I do. I do or I wouldn't spend one date past the time I was sure that I didn't.''

A NINETIES KINDA *Love*

"Not the penthouse?" I joked.

"Not yet, but I'm getting there." Allison Harvey didn't joke as she pressed the elevator button and the whisper-quiet elevator glided upward toward the eighteenth floor, five floors below the penthouse.

Allison was earnestly saying how some of the apartments on her floor cost more than the penthouse because they were bigger. She was cheerful as we rode ever-so-smoothly upward in an elevator paneled with two shades of the kind of gleaming wood that was used on the dashboards in older Mercedeses and Jaguars.

Her eyes teased—not quite smiling, not quite serious. Her skin was free of blemishes and makeup. What she had called a short, maintenance-free, wispy hairdo framed her round race. She may have been slightly overweight as a teenager, but she was trimmed down now.

Her apartment was not huge, but it was large enough for someone who lived alone. In New York terms it would be called a comfortable one-bedroom in a luxury rental, with a twenty-four-hour doorman/concierge, and a state-of-the-art health and fitness club containing a fifty-foot pool.

Nothing was out of place in the living room. It was paneled partially in oak and partially with wall carpeting that was light enough to make it look more spacious than it was.

"Let's not mention the school," she said, "because there aren't all that many black folk who majored in classics at a place like that, and so it would be possible for some people to guess who I am, and then they would know more than I'd want them to know," she said.

Allison Harvey worked for a very diversified, very high-end financial management firm providing a variety of money-management services to entertainers, sports superstars, and an assorted list of very wealthy clients.

"Neither the man I love nor the man I see, let's call him the man I see, knows I'm giving an interview on love. I'll tell them or not tell them, depending on how it comes out. Not that we aren't all very open with each other. I'm sure they would approve as long as our real names are not used."

"I always disguise the identities so people won't be reluctant to be candid. We can call the man you love James, okay? And the man you see, Robert. James and Robert," I said. She took my coat and disappeared with it.

"The names are not important," she agreed. "What is important is how life is conducted for African-American people like us in New York who travel in the rarefied circles where the three of us travel."

"I'll describe James as an artist without saying what art he practices. I'll describe your and Robert's profession, but not in enough detail for anyone to know for sure that it's you," I said.

"Okay, fine," she said. I had been referred to her by a white guy named Seymour Davidoff, who worked as an accountant for one of the clients of her firm.

He had been impressed by her beauty and "sophisticated sizzle. Allison's hot," he had said. I had asked Sy and he guessed that she probably earned about $130,000 a year and that she was about thirty years old.

When black people first broke into the mainstream in significant numbers back in the 1960s and early 1970s, they used to brag about earning the number of thousands of dollars equal to their age.

In the 1980s there was talk about being able to double your age. Allison was above four times her age, if he was correct. "So I guess you earn about a hundred fifty thousand dollars per year."

"About that," she said.

Sy had gone to dinner with her a couple of times but had not made any headway, and so he became her friend. He sometimes invited her to things.

Now speaking of her and James and Robert, she said: "It's very different from the way most black people live, from the way that most people live, but when you consider it, it all makes perfect sense—given who the three of us are."

In the course of talking she poured wine for both of us and we talked about the most-people-would-kill-for view of New York from both the living room and the bedroom of her apartment.

"So love. You want to know about love?" she asked.

"Uh-huh."

"Love is tied to a lot of things for me. I'm playing in a very hard game and the kind of lover I have is a fringe benefit of being in the kind of life I'm in. And the man I see is important to business, as well as to the personal needs I have that one usually thinks of as being fulfilled by love."

"You manage love like you manage money," I said, being very careful to make sure there was no sarcasm in my voice.

"Love is a deal for me, and if the man doesn't bring enough to the table, then there's no deal. You'd better bring some phenomenal something because I'm bringing something phenomenal. I am phenomenal. I'm not reluctant to say that. I am."

The way she chose to live showed how much she valued herself. At our first scheduled meeting at Clarion, a stylish restaurant on the Upper East Side, she wore a double-breasted trouser suit with a herringbone design. It looked like it might have cost a thousand bucks.

Today Allison was wearing a beige wool blazer and a pleated

chocolate-colored long skirt. I noticed that she was not the kind who kicked off her boots when she got home, at least not with me there. The trendy-looking boots were about the same color as the parquet floor.

"The man I love intimidates me a little; I can honestly say that. Whereas I intimidate the man I see. I like both of those feelings. I am with this man who is a masochist. He likes being intimidated by me. He loves me, whereas the man I love has enough money and fame to intimidate a lot of people—not that I'm a masochist, because it doesn't even hurt me that the man I love dates other women. We're all three very civilized people," she laughed.

"You and James and Robert." I sipped more dry red wine.

"I don't mind hearing about their other dates sometimes, not in a weird or perverse way, but if it comes up in the course of conversation we can be very open with each other. I don't need exclusivity to make me feel special."

I asked her about things like jealousy and commitment and wanting someone to be yours and yours alone. She was serious in dismissing these considerations. "What are we talking about here?"

"Love."

"Then, let's talk about what the word means to me, which is not the generally held concept of I-won't-date-anybody-else-if-you-don't. Love in its purest form does not have to include that.

"The man I love knows how to please me, and before him I was impossible to please. He is a lady's man. He knows how to handle ladies on an international scale. He's mastered the things that are the keys to all women. He has interesting things to say and he knows how to listen.

"I like to talk to him about my career, my future. He doesn't judge, but he will tell you what he thinks the outcome will be for something that you might be doing or thinking. He's marvelous that way. He's very successful and he's like a teacher, a mentor, a lover who is teaching me the things I need to know about life.

"When he's in New York, I see him. He likes to have me on his arm at some very important occasions and this helps in my career. I like going to his place. I like being there. He lives in a fabulous building over by the United Nations. A lot of very famous people live in that building. Whenever I go over to his place there is always some reminder of something fantastic that he is involved with.

"And making love to him is wonderful because he is so experienced and because we have this powerful spiritual connection. I usually can't turn my mind off during lovemaking, and so that usually inhibits my enjoyment when I'm making love, but with him that doesn't matter because with him my mind is fully engaged in the act of love so it doesn't have to turn off. Everything that comes into my mind is appropriate to the occasion and so I could say it or act it out—nothing weird, just act out the way I am, express that in the act of love, and that liberates me from the way I am.

"He is a very considerate lover, but at the same time there is this wildness about him that takes over. It's the only time when I can say that I am not afraid to be out of control."

Allison's eyes sparkled and she talked more excitedly when she spoke of his fame and the things that fame brought him, and how truly famous people live in another world, and that she loved him because he took her to that world, and she found that she belonged there.

We finished our wine and she poured more. She talked about how James called her from different places just to talk over things that happened to him. She loved it when she heard from him. She loved living with the knowledge that sooner or later he would call.

"When he's out of the city I do things for him not even thinking about the cost. I run around like a little errand girl. I don't have to think about the cost because whatever I do for him is perfect because of who he is and who I am. He knows who I am. He knows what I am comfortable doing, and so everything he wants me to do is something that I like to do. That's a perfect deal.

"He's not my client, but I give him lots of free advice, and when there is financial stuff in which he's involved actively, I do all sorts of checking for him. I've even gone with his lawyers to meetings for him.

"Will I ever be in love in the other sense? Love as being kind and considerate and patient and enduring and selfless and giving and unconditional and forgiving and nonjudgmental and sensitive? I've never been any of those things.

"I can't say that I've ever wanted to be all those things to anyone, because I do judge and I'm not that patient, and, hell, I'm not that forgiving. If you've done something wrong, I don't forgive. I use that to leverage you for something I want. I want to say I love in that way, but with me there are too many strings attached to it, except with James, more than anyone, all of those strings are removed mostly because those strings never come into play with him.

"The more I think of it, the more I think the answer is no. I won't ever fall in love in that other sense. The closest I think I can come to finding that ultimate passion for someone is James. I believe in him. I have an absolute confidence in him because he is truthful, and that is something that I lack.

"For example, he forces me to be honest. For example, he made me face the issues in my life, and that's something that I had never done, and so I want more of that. I want to face those issues because I learned that true freedom cannot come unless I am totally honest about myself.

"For example, he made me face the fact that all during college I had wanted to be white. I had wanted to fit in so badly that I actually wanted to be white. I had a white boyfriend at college who I really didn't like, but he liked me and that gave me a connection to the world that I felt excluded from at college—the Waspy New England world where people lived next door to the heirs to this fortune or the heirs to that fortune.

"I wanted that world, and so that goes back to my selfishness because when I met James after college and I began wanting what he represented, I didn't want my white boyfriend anymore, which proved that I didn't love him because I didn't care what happened to him, which again goes back to my selfishness.

"I felt joy when I told him I didn't want to see him again. I felt so liberated from wanting to be something I could never be, and because of James I didn't want to be that anymore because I found something else that I wanted to be. Wow! This was great.

"I can say that wanting what James had, and he was black, enabled me to admit that I had once wanted to be white. I came to terms with that and it was okay, but if I hadn't switched and wanted what James represented, I never would have admitted how much I once wanted to be white.

"And I could admit it to James because he didn't judge me. He just talked to me about the consequences of that kind of choice. I also could admit that I wanted to be rich at almost any cost, and since he was already rich he couldn't judge me for that. With a man who's done everything, you don't have to have shame and you don't have to be defensive or aggressive about the things that you want to do. You can talk about anything. He was very intuitive about the secret things of my life, many of the things that I tried to hide most."

At Narsai's, a French restaurant on New York's Upper East Side, with perfectly set tables, brightly polished doweled hardwood floors, and elaborate moldings at the top of the waist-high, cherry-wood paneling, topped by handpainted French wallpaper, I thought about how far black people had traveled in the last three decades.

There were no black people here, and our clothes might have been a little too obviously stylish in contrast to the unstylish opulence of the mostly older diners seated at tables that were not close enough for us to hear anyone's conversation. It was a prix fixe restaurant.

I ordered Columbia River caviar and silently laughed at myself. Allison ordered *les escargots aux champignons* (snails in mushrooms).

Her mood was different, more sober than usual, as she spoke about growing up in Teaneck, New Jersey, in a big house with her mother and two sisters, going to private schools from pre-kindergarten, and going off to a prep school that was just as racially exclusive as the New England college she attended.

The thing that she talked about most was her father and mother getting divorced. "I cried a lot at first and I resented my dad for leaving because I thought he was abandoning us. He made a decision that was based completely on himself and he didn't think about us. He worked as a manager for a Fortune 500 company, and he married his white secretary—a secretary, even though my mother was a professional woman with a law degree—God!

"He didn't think about the repercussions of how it would affect me. I was the youngest child and I was a very needy person. I needed my father and I didn't discover until I was in therapy that even when he was home I never had a relationship where I could go to him and let him know how I felt. That was not what my dad was all about. He was not that type of a man.

"I also learned that I made all my boyfriends pay for my father's transgressions against me. I'm not close to my dad. I talk to my dad maybe twice a year and he's right here in the New York area.

"I have a lot of respect for James in a way I couldn't respect my father. My father left us to marry someone else and I don't think I ever forgave him for that. So I can respect James, and that's why the term *sugar daddy* doesn't apply. It's not what he can give me. It's what I can give him—the respect I've never had for a man, and it feels very good to have one man in your life you truly respect. Do you know how rare that is?

"I was attracted to James because he had achieved so much of what I wanted—money—but he had gotten it on a human level by being an artist, not like my father, who had sold his soul to the corporation to get what little he did get, which for him was pretty good.

"James sacrificed on a human level at magnitudes that I could never do. That no one would ever choose to do because most people could never survive that kind of sacrifice, but those who do happen to survive it have something that I would want but I can't take the risk of sacrificing for it. I could never be all the things that his achievements represent. I could never be all that, and so I wanted to live that vicariously through him, by being in love with him.

"Last summer he had me meet him in Paris and this was the first time I had been to Paris in over three years. I had been there several times as a child and I was there during college with my white boyfriend, and it was a very awkward time because I was not sufficiently grateful for his making it possible for me to be there, or something. I don't know exactly what it was, but he had to do little things to make it seem that I was not used to European refinements—like a bidet, or like the fact that this French impressionist lived in this way and that one in that way—stuff like that. He wanted to show off as the refined one, showing this little black girl European culture. I resented it.

"Anyway, at that time I was the me I used to be—defensive and always eager to argue to defend my turf. So, of course, the guy got on my nerves. His overbearing attitude brought out my intolerance. His arrogance created animosity between us the entire time, but with James it was like magic. He had been to Paris many times, but it was like we were discovering a new enchanted city, both of us, for the first time.

"He was charming and considerate. He was charismatic, even to people who did not know who he was at first. People were drawn to him and he was very good at pushing me into the spotlight so that I just glowed. Things we saw in Paris brought out things about me that he was happy to discover. We held hands. We ran.

We sat in small cafés and bistros, exchanging intimate thoughts about each other.''

Allison and I ate for a while without speaking. The food was excellent. The wine, which Allison had chosen, complemented the meal perfectly.

"When I am with him I feel liberated from all the things that I don't like about myself, because I'm not an easy person to love. I am selfish and I am judgmental. I feel superior. I have this sense of entitlement—a sense of elitism, a sense of exclusivity. I don't belong with ordinary people. I feel that. I feel like I should be adored because I'm just worth it. And those are very selfish things.

"I'm greedy. I always want things. I always crave for more. I'm always looking for better. I want more of things than anyone else around me. I can't stop at enough. I have to have more. I want the convertible Mercedes. I want the closet full of Giorgio Armani suits. I want the assortment of Piaget and Cartier watches. I want to be seen in these things because they confirm my sense of elitism. I'm greedy and it's hard for people to love greedy people.

"It's distasteful. It's not a pure quality. I'll never fall in love because I'll always be looking out for myself. I mean, love is all about the other person, isn't it? It's unconditional and it's enduring and it's patient and kind and considerate and joyful, and God, those are hard things for me to do. I'm not persevering when it comes to somebody else. Love is not boastful, it's not conceited, and those things I am.''

We planned to meet for lunch and talk about Robert, the man who loved her, who was almost like her boss. He was not in her chain of command, but he was on a higher level than she was in the company where she worked.

I had been introduced to Robert once when I came to pick her up from work. I thought then that she had made a point to introduce us and to imply that we were closer friends than we really were. I also noticed that instead of going to Robert's office, she called for Robert to come to her office. "There's someone I want you to meet."

Dutifully, Robert came, smiling. He was as she described him, handsome, with a very gentle face. He was very trim—his weight, his hair, his mustache, his white shirt. He wore blue suspenders, which picked up one of the colors in his multicolored necktie.

She left us alone to talk for a while. He was very friendly in the inconsequential kind of way that many of the guys who went to Harvard Business School are friendly. Charming. Always gracious, but you can sense their minds at work, always in search of the best practical outcome in any line of conversation.

I put a few things out there for him to work with. He seemed to come to the conclusion that I wanted him to reach: I was not a person whom he was likely ever to do business with, and I was not a contender for Allison's affections. He relaxed a little.

After we talked for a while Allison returned. "Take care of Allison, she's a very special lady," he said finally.

"I have two tendencies in me, according to James. One is a tendency to dominate. The other tendency is to be babied, to be adored, adored like you wouldn't believe. That's where Robert comes in. He adores me."

"Then, why don't you just be with him and that would be love?" I said as I ordered penne and sundried tomatoes.

She ordered ricotta dumplings and sweet roasted peppers.

"Why should I?" she said as another waiter poured San Pellegrino water into our stemware. "He is one hell of a selfish person. He is so unbelievably selfish, but there is a part of me that's attracted to that because it gets to be a contest of who can be more selfish.

"He can be very giving because out of my selfish nature I can coerce him to give because he's a very fearful man. He's very vulnerable. He's intimidated easily. He's very intelligent, but he's emotionally retarded, very much so. He clings to things that have happened to him in the past and he can't get around them.

"And he lets people emotionally beat on him. And on a sick level, I beat up on him and it's brought me what I want. All I have to do is beat on him emotionally. He has brought me to the attention of the guys higher up in the company.

"For example, they wanted someone who had a degree in psychology, and he told them to try me because my undergraduate degree was in psychology. Of course it wasn't, but he told them that and the number-one guy called me in and I gave him a really helpful briefing, which put me in at the decision-making, policy-making level, because now when the big guys brainstorm they call me in.

"They love me. I enjoy this kind of work—the psychology of money and people with money. In the company people don't know that Robert and I see each other.

"Also, the odd thing is that the people in the company think that Robert is very tough, very cold—you know, the old black street-smart, tough cliché. They think he's a killer. They brought him in as the fourth-highest guy in the company because they wanted him to clean house, to fire some people."

"And he's not tough enough to do it," I said, seeing if I could anticipate her. We were eating our meals now.

"Oh, he'll fire them as long as the three guys at the top rally around him and give him little slogans about effectiveness, competitiveness, about doing what is better for the greater good of the company.

"But they don't know that I am very helpful to him on this score, because I can intimidate him into firing these guys by telling him he's a weak person whenever he begins to find some value in the person that he has to fire.

"For example, there were two guys who'd been there for thirty years and they didn't even know how to log in to some of the advance data services. At first, Robert said he would teach them, and so he brought in this very attractive consultant, hoping that they would do it just because she was so attractive, and they told him that they didn't want to learn how to type. That's what they called working with a computer—typing.

"I just told him that he was weak and that he didn't have the mental toughness to hang in there during the lawsuits that they might bring. I said he didn't have the mental stamina and tenacity to make it work. 'You're chicken and all you do is go fetch the stick that Don Marcus and Conrad Oldmyer are going to have to use, and if they have to use it themselves, the next thing they're going to do is use it on your ass.'

"And you know what? He fired the two guys and they didn't sue. Robert turned out to be a hero because I can intimidate him into doing things. The guys took a retirement package, and Robert decided that I was the best thing that ever happened to him. He tells me I'm great. He tells me I'm beautiful. He tells me I'm intelligent. He's glad to be with me."

"Why speak of it in such crass terms? Why not say he needs a little decision-making support and because you love him you give it to him?" I threw in the word *love* to see where she would go with it.

She stuck to her point. "He calls meetings and gives verbatim my solutions to problems. I love that. You're right," she said, responding to the implications of my statement. "I probably won't fall in love. Who wants to fall in love with someone like that?"

"Maybe he is in love," I said. "The question is, do you love him?"

"No way. He's too weak. He led me to believe that he had bought a new Jaguar until I saw the car. It was five years old. I lit into his ass. I love sending him out in the rain to get me something when I'm sick."

"You know you're talking about love—in a way."

"He doesn't do it because he loves me. He's selfish. He does it because I make him do it. Love is a total commitment to something or someone regardless of the price, regardless of the magnitude of the sacrifice that you would make for the loved person or object—completely, one hundred percent, selfless," she said.

"But, then, you demand that he be weak in order that you dominate, and then you can't love him because he's weak."

"You're right. My competitive nature couldn't love someone who's as strong as I am. There would just be too much conflict. Dominating seems to be more important than love. It's very difficult for me being out of control.

"The only situation that I feel comfortable being out of control with is James, because I know he would never misuse me because I'm not important enough to him to get anything out of doing that.

"So he is the only person I would do things for. I give him free investment advice. It's made him a lot of money. I don't ask for anything from it. It's like gambling. Anything that he might give me, I want it to stay in the pot so we can gamble some more. It's the thrill that keeps me going.

"It's like a purpose that is higher than myself. It's the only transcendent purpose that I have in life. It's like a high, watching things happen for him. I am happier with that than I am with anything in my life.

"But Robert—the situation with him is kind of dangerous. I need that thrill to keep me going. It's fun. It's thrilling for me being with him and he's working right there in the office. He's not the person who makes decisions about my career, but he interacts daily with those men, and whenever he throws me the ball, I still have to do an excellent job, but at least I get the ball thrown to me.

"It's thrilling to be there every day and not get caught—to have people know it without being able to prove it. This puts me in the class with this other girl. This white girl who has a thing with the big boss, which everybody knows about but no one can, or would want to, prove. It's like a high.

"I enjoy that, oh, yeah. And Robert likes to have his ass kicked, and at first I didn't do that and all he kept doing was talking about his ex-wife and how she kicked his ass. And now, as he says, 'When I'm with you, she doesn't exist.'

"I know she doesn't. He's too busy enjoying the ass-kicking that I'm giving him—the present ass-kicking rather than the past one.

"I'm his way of escaping from the things in the past that he can't let go of. I keep him busy doing for me because this is what he calls making love to me—doing for me. He might say: 'I'll make you dinner.'

"I'll say: 'No, I want to go out.'

"He'll say: 'Can we watch this movie?' 'Can we go to this show?'

"I'll say: 'No. I want to watch that movie. Hold my coat. Hold my bag.'

"He says: 'Okay, hon.' Right on cue. He might say: 'If I get transferred, will you go to San Francisco with me? You and I will be a team.'

"I say: 'While you're in San Francisco, I'll be here making deals in the big leagues. See you.' He actually enjoys, loves, to have me talk to him like that, but if I didn't treat him like that he'd start telling me about how bad his ex-wife is treating him. God! I know it.

"And also I take his mind off pressures at work. I make sure his mind is on me. Everybody wins. He manages to win. A guy that high doesn't get there by being a total jerk. He's a partial jerk. For example, he knows James, and he knows that I date James, and he thinks that one day I'll get James to invest in one of the deals he might be putting together—and you know what? He's right because he's very good at putting deals together, at hooking important people up together.

"His lack of an ego makes him very good at managing people with big egos. He has an ego, but his ego gratification is invested only in the outcome, not at all in the process. I know he's managing me too. There is not a day that goes by without him telling me that I'm the most beautiful woman he's ever been with, and that's true.

"He never selects the restaurant. He presents the name of the restaurant to me as a suggestion of something that he wants to do for me—take me there—and usually I accept because I like being catered to in that way. And it gives me the option to kick his ass if I don't like the place.

"When we're in the restaurant, he never picks what we eat because I pick two things that I want to eat. Then sometimes he might make a stand. What he calls making a stand is picking what he wants to order, but then if I want to quell his rebellion, all I have to do when my entrée comes is not like it, and set up a hostile atmosphere with the waiter, and to get out of this dilemma he'll let me eat some of what he has, and that makes him feel like a hero.

"He feels like he has saved the day, especially if you put a couple of pleases and thank-yous out there in a soft voice. He'll take up arms against the waiter. He's very funny. I enjoy not enjoying myself with him, which I enjoy.

"Total control. That's the kind of person I am. No one can love a person like me unless I make them love me. No one can fall in love with me because I have to be so much in control and demanding and dominant. It's almost like a disease."

BEING Loved

I love not working, and I love Tom for making it possible for me to live well without working. He goes to his job every day and earns the money. I love him for that. I don't love him for that. I love him; and he loves me enough to say: 'Honey, you don't have to work,' " Honey said with sweetness in her voice. Then she laughed and her face filled with glee. Honey's real name is Maxine.

"I like my house. I like my plants. I love my children. I don't want to be in that stuff that Tom is in. He works for the city. He's an attorney for the city, or, rather, he's an attorney with a law firm retained by the city."

"That's a fantasy for some women," I said, "to be loved so much that someone just says, 'Stay home.' "

"I don't know how many other women would want it. Some women would find it boring. I don't get bored. I don't get bored because I love my own company," she said in a lighthearted way.

"I like doing things by myself when the kids are in school, and then I start my duties when they come home," she said, sitting on a chair in her state-of-the-art country kitchen, complete with red, yellow, white, and green flowered seat cushions on cane-backed chairs around a glass-topped, cane-bottom table. "While they're in school, I go and do things."

"Serve on committees," I said to get her started playing.

"No. But I have served on committees. I just do stuff. San Francisco is a great city for doing stuff." Honey laughed at herself.

"With no purpose in mind?"

"Yes," she pouted playfully, "to share what I do with my husband, when he comes home."

"You two like to talk a lot?"

"We like to talk a lot and he likes to hear what I saw and what I did. I mean, it's not a question to the little wife: 'Dear, how was your day?' It's not like that. It's more like when I see something in the papers that has to do with politics, especially of the city, or something happening in the city, he can talk about that and tell me things about it.

"Then I can talk to him about what went on at the park." Honey laughed, but she was serious. I bet she could say what went on at the park even when she wasn't there. Some days she wasn't there. She was in bed. She admitted that she liked to sleep, not watch television and sleep, not lounge and sleep. Just sleep.

"When the kids come home from school, I'm ready, though. I don't let sleep interfere with my responsibilities," she said and laughed.

I joked. "That's what I've been trying to figure out. Just what are your responsibilities?"

She laughed and pouted.

I could hear the voices of other women:

"Sho-o-ot. Me, not have to work. I would love to have a deal like that. I wish more brothers had their acts together. Does Tom have any brothers?" a junior high school teacher said.

"I don't know if I would feel comfortable depending totally on someone else. I wouldn't have the feeling of independence that I like," a woman who worked in a hospital said.

"I would get bored. I would feel useless. I wouldn't have a purpose to my life. I have to work," said a coworker at the same hospital.

"I don't think I could have it like that. That's not the way men react

to me. More power to her," said a travel agent whose husband didn't work.

"Obviously she knows how to make her husband fall in love with her over and over again, for him to give her everything he possibly can. It's a fantasy life for many women, but it isn't for me. I want my own money, and the chance to do my own thing, occupationally, without the necessity of a man. I want the man—my husband—to complement my life as much as I complement his," said a public school administrator who was not married.

"Thank God I don't have this woman's life. All that I can think of is how empty it sounds," said an unmarried account executive for a Fortune 500 company. *"I'm not saying that everyone should be a supercareer woman, but I do believe every husband and wife should have a meaningful life apart from each other."*

"I have always argued that *love* is a verb. Anyone can say they love you, but it's what they do that counts," I said to Maxine as we sat in her kitchen.

"*Love* is not a verb. *Love* is a noun—a person, place, or thing," Honey said, enjoying her review of elementary school grammar. There is no action that can be performed that proves that someone loves someone. There is no action you can perform to get someone to love you. They either have it or they don't. It's a noun."

"Okay, but what about the guy who has the feeling of love in his heart and every time things don't go his way he abuses his wife?"

"Then, it's not love."

"Okay, okay, wait a minute. Follow my line of questioning." I could see that we were both enjoying our game of cat and mouse. "And what about the woman who has all the love in the world for this guy but still she uses all sorts of underhanded methods . . ."

"It's not love," she said.

"Okay, okay, then, love is an action. What they do to each other and for each other determines if it's love, not the feeling they have for each other, because the man and the woman I just mentioned have the feeling."

"They don't have the feeling. If each of them was honest with himself or herself and honest with each other, they'd both know that they don't have the feeling."

"Or the feeling would produce an action toward the loved one," I said, trying to trap her.

"No. The only thing that love requires is that you be yourself, and if someone loves you you'll know it. If you love someone, they'll know it."

I laughed.

She admitted that she was somewhat disorganized and had a tendency not to finish things; and so it was apparent that she kept herself busy promising to get organized and actually getting started before deciding to do something else instead. Then she corrected herself and said she was not disorganized. "*Disorganized* means that you want to be organized. I am unorganized. There's a big difference."

Sleep might have been one of the things that she did rather than organize. Inactivity may have accounted for the fact that she was overweight, by conventional standards; but she didn't look bad at, maybe, 170 pounds. She was shaped up nice. In fact, she had a cute, plump figure—nothing sloppy. She hadn't let herself go. It seemed that she took good care of herself, even pampered herself.

"No, we don't actually talk a lot. We just spend time together in our home. I'm a homemaker." She laughed again now that she had named her responsibility. "He has things he likes to do. I check the children's homework. If there are problems at school that we can just talk about, I let the kids talk about all this. If someone has to go to school with them, usually it's my husband. If it's something official, he likes to go."

"In the division of labor, shouldn't that be your job?" I tried to get on her case again.

"We don't have a division of labor." She laughed.

I could hear the voices of those same women all over the country:

"This is all very surreal. I will never know of the love she feels for her husband because there is no man who will ever let a woman be more than what he is. And if she does not make him the center of her world, then there are going to be problems. There has to be a division of labor. Her full-time job is to make him feel love," said a secretary for a foreign consulate.

"I must say that I really dislike this woman. She is not someone I would want to know, and certainly not to form any positive relationship with," said the account executive.

"I don't know if I should fear for her," said the public school administrator. "If her husband dies, loses his job, or something else, I wonder how she will continue."

"Is she a red-bone and considers her husband's sacrifice her due," said a schoolteacher who was dark-skinned. "Sounds like everyone is happy— well-adjusted black middle-class family enjoying the American dream."

"This woman needs to start living in the real world with the rest of us," said the travel agent. "I see why Maxine has a tendency not to be able to finish things, or a habit of starting projects only to go on to something else. I can't get a grip on what her role is in her marriage. She seems to have little need to be needed."

"I agree that love is a noun," said another schoolteacher. "It is a feeling, but it needs an action to validate it. Love is as love does. It's a force. It can be both a creative force and/or a destructive force."

"Self-centered? Selfish?" asked a woman who worked at an ad agency.

"I think someone in here is lying. Maybe both of them are lying. People live lies. They live illusions. Some illusions last a short time and others last a long time, but reality has to be faced. If someone isn't working, then someone is using someone, and someone is allowing themselves to be used for reasons of their own," said a woman who called herself a realist.

"White men do shit like that. It's a trick. That's how they make persons into nonpersons. That's why there is so much anger in the women's movement coming from women who once seemed to have had it made, or whose mothers had what Maxine has."

"This woman is a ditz."

"Love is a verb. It's a situational verb. Love is also an adjective. It describes a euphoric feeling that one might experience for a moment or a certain period of time. Our society is not designed for love to be a noun."

"What's your job?" I asked playfully. We were still in her kitchen enjoying coffee.

"Just being myself. That's why he married me, because of who I am. He likes spending weekends with his family."

"Do you plan the weekends?"

"No, he likes to plan them. You're just trying to start trouble," she said.

"Consciousness-raising in the area of rights and responsibilities."

"That's what he's into all day, rights and responsibilities. He doesn't want that when he get's home. He wants to be loved. He wants love," she said, letting herself fall into the *love*-as-a-verb trap.

"And what does that entail?"

"It doesn't entail anything," she laughed as she jumped out of the trap. "It's just knowing that I have love for him."

"In your heart?" I asked. "But how does he know?"

"He knows. When you're loved, you know. When someone

has love for you, you know. When people meet him, they know he's loved, that someone has love for him," she laughed. "You can look at someone and tell if they're loved."

"Are there some people who don't know when they're loved?"

"If they don't know, then, they're not loved. Part of loving someone is the gift of their knowing that they are loved. And part of loving is being able to be loved."

The same voices of women that I heard before:

"I think that there are some people who cannot be loved, because of what they think of themselves. In fact, I don't think many people can be loved. Bob Marley has this song 'Could you be loved?' I listened to the song one day and concluded that I couldn't, in all honesty."

"Maxine's biggest act of love is her presence," said the school admin-istrator, who liked Maxine and previously expressed fear for her if her husband should ever die. "I'm not sure, but I would imagine that Tom's act of love is to provide, an act that is altogether well received, an act that could not be well received by many women, even ones who say they could. They couldn't."

"I know the Bob Marley song. I used to sing it to myself and I came to the conclusion that if you are not loved, can you love? And if you can't love, then, how can you be loved? I'd have to say no. So Maxine definitely provides a service: because she can be loved, she makes it possible for her husband to love and, therefore, to be loved."

"Would you love him if he wasn't making the kind of money that can make all this possible without you having to work?"

"When I was working, I couldn't love anyone," she said. She said she had been working at a health-maintenance company. She said it was an okay job. The problem was that her mind was always on her job, and she said she knows now that for her to love, she has to have her mind free. "Your life will be dominated by whatever you keep your attention on. I kept my attention on complaints that people had about the service they got from our associated physicians. I could not love. I could not be loved.

"I took a year off and I learned how to be happy with myself, and how to be happy in the world with all the good things there are to do. San Francisco is a great city for this. The climate is wonderful. San Francisco is a very self-confident city. It is not trying to be anything that it is not.

"I used to drive down the Pacific Coast Highway to Half Moon Bay or sometimes all the way down to Monterey. I was never in a hurry to get somewhere geographically or psychologically, but spiritually, so it didn't matter where I was.

"I used to go to the Japanese Tea Garden and just talk to people. I love the bonsai trees and the wooden bridge and the reflecting pools. The Palace of Fine Arts. North Beach. Angel's Island, the symphony—you name it.

"Now it's not that I can talk about those things; it's that my life has been deepened by the enjoyment of those things. Not *deepened,* because that is a somber word. My life has been enlivened by those things.

"I don't need to talk about them to my husband or my children; they are just a part of the me that I share with my family. I used to go down to Chinatown and just look at the shops where they have hundreds of hand-carved statues. For the first time I took time to notice the expressions on the faces of some of those statues.

"I began eating a lot of different kinds of food and really learning to savor and enjoy the taste of different foods. That's why I say San Francisco is such a great city.

"I created a regime for myself—what kind of body massage I liked, what kinds of perfumes I like wearing. For example, I knew

I loved getting my nails done, not just because that made me look nice, but I actually like the sensation of someone pushing my cuticles back with an emery board. Things like that.

"I learned everything I could about how my body works. I learned how to cure myself with my mind, just by concentrating on how various parts of my body functioned.

"There was something that I used to do quite consciously. This was a time when those little yellow happy faces were very popular, and I thought about the fact that there are people who could put a smile on their faces anytime they wanted to.

"I learned how to put a smile on my insides. I could actually picture my insides smiling. I called it smiling internally. I could actually feel that my insides were doing something that corresponded to those little yellow happy faces.

"No one can put a smile on their faces all the time, and I couldn't put a smile on my insides all the time, nor would I want to, but I learned how to do it as often as the most efficient receptionist could put one on her face. I greeted everything with an internal smile.

"I learned what kind of activities I enjoyed. For example, I learned that I really like to drive. I loved driving not as a means of getting to someplace but just as a means of seeing things passing by and going to different places just to be there and enjoy being there.

"There were a lot of little things about me that I knew I enjoyed but I was too busy searching for what I was supposed to enjoy—a relationship.

"I learned not to need those head-over-heels love affairs that I had been having since high school. I remember I was in love with this boy in high school and I thought I couldn't live without him. I used to wait for him outside the lunchroom because I had to eat lunch with him. I used to wait for him after school because I wanted him to walk me home. I spent half the night talking to him on the phone. I was miserable when he didn't call when he said he was going to call.

"I got dumped by him and then I found somebody else, and someone else, and several someone elses. It was the same with all of them. I worked very hard at trying to make these relationships work. I worked very hard at trying to get these men to love me, or at least like me, but I kept messing up.

"It wasn't their fault. I just couldn't do the right thing and I was miserable because I needed a relationship to make my life complete.

"I remember this one love affair. I loved this guy to death. I was a real good-intentioned fool. He had a way of making me feel sympathy for him, and that way I would spend all my time thinking of what to do next to try to make him like me.

"I did his homework. I did his laundry. I ran errands for him. I was happy to do it, so I told myself. The only thing I wasn't happy about was that no matter what I did it came out wrong. I don't mean he took it wrong. I did it wrong. I was a classic fuck-up. I was always misplacing things, and forgetting to do things, and showing up at the wrong place, or at the wrong time.

"He was always screaming at me. Things got so confused. I'm smart, but my mind was always somewhere else, so I fucked things up. He ran off with a girl who didn't do anything for him. I didn't blame him. I was a fuck-up. I didn't want to be, but I was.

"I continued that pattern after college and I was getting bitter at men, but mostly depressed at myself and at life. Then, when I took the year off, I discovered that if I spent my time trying to make something happen, I am more likely to mess it up than not. Seriously.

"On that level nothing I did was ever right. And so I began working on another level—is my heart in the right place? Is my head in the right place? Am I sincere? That's when I learned how to make my insides smile.

"I worked at what I could work at successfully. I worked at myself. I worked on the spiritual level. That was the level on which I could work without fucking things up.

"And then I met this man, Tom, and something in me was drawn to him. You know how there are some things that you can't pass them without reaching out and touching them, and even when you don't want to touch them you want to be in their presence.

"And when you're not in their presence, you can still feel their presence inside of you where the happy face used to be, and every time you think of them you smile because of the way they are.

"That's how it was with him. He would call me up and I would fall asleep on the phone while he was talking and he didn't mind at all. It was the strangest thing.

"When I'd hear from him the next day he'd say, 'I wasn't talking about anything anyway.' He thought it was cute that I used to fall asleep on him. He thought that nearly everything I did was cute.

"This was back when there was no time cost for local calls, and sometimes we would both fall asleep and not hang up the phone until the morning.

"My family couldn't understand it. They would say, 'You were talking to that man all night,' and I would say yes because I knew they thought I was a little weird anyway, so I couldn't tell them that we would both fall asleep with the phones off the hook.

"Tom and I could be together or not be together, but we were together anyway. He said he liked his job more because he could think about me at work and people would see him smiling and being positive and they liked him more.

"I was running low on money, so I went back to work, and we couldn't figure out what was wrong. I had to focus on other things and so I couldn't smile inside all the time, and Tom said he couldn't feel me in the same way.

"We talked and talked for a long time because I was doubtful, but he said he wanted to marry me and he wanted me to have his babies and raise them to be as happy as we were. So that was that.

"Our marriage has not been a bed of roses. We've had our share of problems, but we never thought that more money, by my going to work, would solve those problems.

"I never thought that being involved in a career would make things better. Life has its ups and downs, and we kept in mind that we had ways to face those ups and downs that suited the two of us.

"When we have problems we don't blame each other. We just accept the fact that we have to live through whatever it is. I know that my job is to try to stay in a happy mood as much as I can. Sometimes I have to work at it, and then when he comes home I ask: 'Did you miss me?' I make him say it. He doesn't like to come right out and say it. He likes me to get him to say it.

"I break into the conversation at a certain time and make him say it, and that's how he forgets about whatever it is that he was talking about, which he didn't really want to be talking about anyway. It was just like when I used to fall asleep on him. It would make him realize that what he was talking about or worrying about or complaining about didn't matter as much as he thought it did. Oh, well."

" 'Did you miss me?' You'd make him answer."

"Yes, I'd break into the conversation at a point that makes him laugh. He'd be talking about something really serious and it would not be a matter of me not listening to him. I'd listen, but then I always know right when to say 'Did you miss me?' And he'd shake his head and laugh. 'Of course. Of course.' And he'll just stop thinking about it."

*   *   *

That was Maxine's story. The next thing I wanted to do was interview Tom. I met him one day and we had lunch down on Lombard Street.

"Your problem," said her husband, Tom, the lawyer who litigated for the city of San Francisco, "is that you look at love as if it is something that someone gives you, and something that you give someone in return, like an exchange of goods."

Since he was a litigator, I expected him to say, "Is that not true, Mr. Davis?"

He didn't, but I confessed. Then I added: "Your wife must have told you that I was trying to catch her in a trap."

He leaned forward. He had a robust laugh, and he was careful to be very friendly to balance the fact that he was very aggressive. "What in particular are you looking for?"

"What is love?" I asked.

"Love is a feeling you have in your heart relative to another person."

"You and your wife didn't collaborate on your answers, did you, Counselor?" I imitated a cross-examiner.

"We collaborate on everything." He laughed his robust laugh. "We collaborate on everything. You didn't think you were going to get a different story, did you?"

"Then, it is not a verb, an action?"

"It's a thing that colors all your actions not just toward the person but toward everything, when you have love in your life." He laughed. I knew he didn't see a way I could get around his comprehensive statement.

"You guys are ganging up on me."

"We gang up on everything. Love is a thing, the possession of which brings joy into your life. Maxine and I love each other, but it's best for me to speak only for myself. I love her."

"And that's why she doesn't have to work?"

"What would her working bring into my life? What would I have? She's a college graduate. Maybe sixty to seventy thousand dollars a year more income, but I wouldn't love her if she worked. She would be another person. Life is about balance. More money wouldn't bring more happiness into my life. She, being who she really is, does."

"Would she work to support both of you?"

"Then we'd both have to be different people, so, no, I don't think so. I couldn't deal with that, being who I am. But let me cover the points you've raised one at a time. If I die I have insurance. She won't have to work. I've got a three-quarter-of-a-million-dollar insurance policy, double indemnity.

"Some people are created for careers, but I don't think everyone is. That's just the way they advertise it in America, that you're not worth anything unless you're dedicated to IBM.

"She is not my shadow. She is a very independent person. I want her in my life in a certain way, so I make that possible. Life exists on many levels. I work on the material level to make us happy. She works on the spiritual level to make us happy.

"I think I enjoy my work as much as she enjoys hers. That's the division of labor."

Love IN GREENER GRASS

I hadn't read the story in a long time, but I don't mind reading it now. It's the story of our love back when my husband was in the army twenty years ago, and everything my then-husband said about our love back then was true back then, so why not read it now? It's the truth even though that truth changed.

"It doesn't hurt to read it. It's more that we were both kids then. We started going together when I was fourteen and he was seventeen. We were both a couple of kids. He was the only man I had ever been with. We got married when I was seventeen because he was going in the army and I knew I couldn't live without him, so we got married so I could go with him.

"We had that very, very, very deep feeling that you have when you're in love at that age. So what he said was true for that time.

"The love story I am referring to is "A Love Affair," and it was the truth based on interviews with my husband that was printed as the first story in *Love, Black Love*.

"So I agree. His words represented both of our feelings back then. Back then I couldn't live without him and he couldn't live without me. We couldn't go on without each other. We couldn't wait until I graduated high school so we could get married. It was wonderful.

"We got married and the story that my husband told represented the first years of our marriage. Back in 1978 he said, and I quote: 'I was stationed in Fort Knox, Kentucky, as a radio operator

147

in an armored battalion. We didn't have a car, so I hitched back and forth from where we lived, in Louisville, Kentucky, to Fort Knox, which was thirty-four miles away. We were in the field sometimes for weeks in the dead of winter. She was in the apartment alone, no friends, no money, half the time no food, pregnant.

" 'I remember the time when we had one can of sardines to eat. I didn't want to eat it, because she was pregnant and I wanted her to have it, and she didn't want to eat it, because I had to go out in the field in the cold and she wanted me to have it.

" 'No furniture. We sat on the floor and played pitty-pat and whoever lost would have to eat the sardines—whoever lost. I lost but I wouldn't eat them.'

"I know that my husband also told a story about how he not only loved me but how he learned how to make love to me, which was true. The sex was good. He was right about that. He said:

" 'She gets on top sometimes, but not much. We try fancy stuff sometimes, but neither one of us likes it better than plain, ordinary lovin'.

" 'That's another reason I know she loves me. When we first got married I didn't have the experience to wait for her to reach a climax. I was ashamed sometimes, because I knew she wasn't getting satisfaction, but she never said anything bad about it to me. She put up with it.

" 'Then I talked to this preacher, when we were having some trouble in our marriage, and he told me the story of Jacob and the angel. Jacob started wrestling with the angel like at eight o'clock one night, and after a while the angel said, "Jacob, Jacob, let me go," and Jacob said, "Angel, I will not let you go until you bless me."

" 'And so Jacob continued wrestling with the angel until, say, ten o'clock, and then the angel said, "Jacob, Jacob, let me go." And Jacob said, "I will not let you go until you bless me."

" 'And so Jacob continued wrestling with the angel until midnight, and the angel said, "Jacob, Jacob, let me go," and Jacob said, "I will not let you go until you bless me."

" 'This continued until dawn, and then the preacher said that the Scriptures said that great rivers of water flowed down on Jacob. He said that this was the way a woman was. You had to be with her until her river flowed. This is how he explained the female reaching climax. After then I learned how to bless my angel, and make my angel bless me.'

"My husband was a very sweet man. I admit this, but what you have to remember is that he was my first boyfriend. We were high school sweethearts. It's only natural. You got to look at what's going on here. I wanted to check other things out and so did he. It would be natural later on to want to check things out. See, you got to really look at that.

"The marriage had been on the line for ten years. I think it began coming apart right after he got out of the service. But we agreed that we had three children to support and our goal was to see them graduated from high school, and when the last one did in 1988 we agreed that we would go our separate ways. We both agreed neither one of us had to push.

"While he was in the service there was only the two of us and the children. He had a world—the army—and I was a camp follower, a military wife who worked to make ends meet because he didn't make enough money to support us, but basically I belonged to him.

"If the military moved him, I had to move with him. While he was in the service I had to go to eight different colleges to get enough college credits to graduate. You see what I mean?

"So then we got out of the service. Now we're in a different world. There's no more 'your little world.' Now we're out in the working world. When we broke up I had just started my career, and we were both bitter, and I had a point to prove—that I would be successful—so I didn't really want to be married. The only thing that I was looking to do was to be successful. That's what happened. That's all that happened. I think it was also because we hadn't had experiences with others.

"I saw men that I thought were attractive. I couldn't talk to them. He saw women that he thought were attractive, I'm sure. He couldn't talk to them. Because of these values. We weren't the messing-around kind. That's not how we grew up. So we were definitely set on the only way this could happen was to get a divorce.

"From 1980 to 1987, seven years, I woke up hundreds of mornings thinking: Oh! My God, I can't believe this. I've never slept with anyone else. You talk to your girlfriends and they say this man is this way and that one is that way. You know the shit?

"We had been together too long and we had not grown be-cause of that. We had not grown. He was the only man I had ever gone to bed with. That's all. And to see if someone else found me sexy or attractive. Believe me, when the divorce happened neither one of us cried.

"I still love him. If he ever had a problem, I would be there for him. If I ever had a problem, he would be there for me, bottom line. We have three children together, and we both love the chil-dren and the children love both of us. There was never much of an argument about that.

"We still get together for family occasions. He doesn't have another wife and I don't have another husband, but we don't try to work out a reconciliation.

"It was just that he was my first experience. Number one, okay, like I said, we got married young, at seventeen. We hadn't dealt with anyone else, and in the dark I would have fantasies, but you can't touch it, because we had these values that are old-fashioned. So the only thing we could do is be angry at each other for what each of us couldn't do because of the other.

"And just even in my mind, to sleep with another man, even in my mind, when I'm married, would make me feel like nothing. So I didn't do it. But there were people that I fantasized about, that's only normal. So I really think that had everything to do with it.

"I know that it wasn't to get back at him. I didn't do it because he once cheated on me in the marriage and I never cheated on him.

"I knew he cheated because he once had lipstick on the sleeve of his shirt. He was in the reserves and he used to go away during the summer. And the bottom line was he used to go away and he came back from St. Louis, where he had been for two weeks.

"We were living out in Harvey, Illinois, just south of Chicago, at the time. And when he came back from St. Louis, and suddenly I got this infection, and I went to the doctor and the doctor said it was transferred to me.

"The doctor said that you could get it from a swimming pool, but he didn't swim and swimming pools don't wear lipstick. I didn't accuse him of sleeping with someone, but I did open up my medical book: it's called "the bug" and you can get it in the swimming pool, but the guilt and his reaction, he didn't get it through the swimming pool.

"He was happy I didn't jump all over his case. Like 'Oh, my God, I hope she doesn't want the details.' I didn't want the details. I knew he was sorry he did it. That was enough. We were married and I am old-fashioned, and I do think that men and women are different. I do think there is a double standard, and, bottom line, I don't have any problem with that.

"That happened about eight years before I left him. I don't think he ever did it again. I don't know. I didn't ever worry about it.

"I didn't leave him because there was someone else I wanted to deal with. I hadn't seen someone I really wanted to be with. Our children were grown and so, bottom line, it all came down to experience.

"In the ten years since me and my husband have been apart,

I have met other men. Let's say I've enjoyed learning the ways of other men. For a while I was looking to other men for the kind of love that I had in marriage, but I got cured of that. This guy named Gregory cured me.

"When I was going with Greg there were two men—one black, Greg; and one white, Bill Conway, William R. Conway. I'm not like a lot of black women. I don't, and didn't, have a problem dating a white guy. I didn't worry about people looking at us when Bill and I went somewhere.

"I liked Bill, and I could have defied society and been with him if that's what I wanted. But I say that and yet my children don't know anything about him. They never met him. My family didn't know anything about him, but I did introduce them to Greg.

"I used to tell myself that I didn't introduce them to Bill because there were some other problems and we both recognized them. But I think the real reason was he was white.

"And when I found myself getting used to the way he was and feeling that I could live with a man like that, I'd always think of these problems.

"Cocaine was one problem. Both Bill and Greg were into co-caine. And with both of them there was a sexual problem, so it's not a matter of a sexual stereotype that Bill didn't measure up because he's white. That's not true because I had the same problem with both of them.

"I'm not making excuses. It was just not coming up . . . you know what I mean? Like, as much as it should. Well, to be with either Bill or Greg permanently, as in love and marriage, I would have had to accept oral sex.

"Bill treated me like a doll, that's cool, and I used to have a very, very good time with him, but sexually I knew there was a problem. He knew there's a problem. He said it.

"He said he knew I would leave him in a year or two. Because in a year or two he would be impotent. He was secure enough to say that. White guys are much more secure in talking frankly about themselves sexually; black guys are more into pretense.

"This is what Bill said quite cheerfully: 'You still have a big sexual desire and I don't desire it all that much.' A black guy would never admit that.

"Bill is very wealthy and so he doesn't have a lot of guilt or insecurity about who he is and what he does. That's the main reason why I liked being with him. I could relax more. I didn't always have to make him feel like a man, or to make him feel all right about anything he was doing.

"He snorted his coke and he drank bourbon, did his marijuana, and that, coupled with his working, he was totally into oral sex just to be able to do something for me.

"He's very aggressive. Working around the clock? He's a partner in a law firm down on LaSalle Street. So he's there at eight in the morning and he might be there till twelve at night. Because money excites him. You know, making money for that business. That's what excites him, bottom line.

"Sometimes when he gets home early—eight o'clock at night is early for him—he might call and ask if I want to have dinner. He might not want to go out, but he orders in the best and then after dinner he might say: 'If you wanta watch this movie, you can stay right here in the living room and watch it, here's your robe, but I have to go to bed, because I have to leave at six in the morning and I have to get up and write this report, and when you finish watching TV you can get into bed and go to sleep if you want.'

"I could do anything I wanted. He has a beautiful place down on Lake Shore Drive. You know what I'm saying. I could get everything I wanted except the kind of sexual attention I wanted. He was excited about money, not sex.

"I can do without sex. Apparently I'm doing without it now, if you know what I mean. Come on. But, then again, am I making excuses, maybe I wasn't attracted to him really. You know what I mean.

"He's an attractive man. Don't get me wrong. I think it had something to do with the color. Because whites do come in different colors. And he has blue eyes and white hair. He's very well fit in weight. Height is nice—six feet two. He's a handsome guy. I can see in his younger days he was very handsome. But he had that kind of color that wouldn't tan.

"Whether he loved me or not I don't know, but he was fascinated by my color. He treated me like I was a goddess or something. He looked up to me in a personal aspect.

"If he hadn't liked me, he wouldn't put up with me. He could get other women. White women are crazy about him, but I think he just likes black women. The woman he had before me was black.

"At his apartment, he has black art on the walls, and he did a lot of things that are black in terms of entertainment. He liked to go to the blues clubs. He loved jazz. He loved black food. He loved greens.

"He's from down South. A lot of the Southern guys like black stuff. He might be black. You know what I mean? There's just so much stuff about him that's black in this white skin. But he's versatile too. Sometimes he'll take you to very elegant places, sometimes he likes to go to hole-in-the-wall clubs—only sometimes. He's definitely a hip person.

"But his mannerisms are white. He's very charming—not like black men are not—but he'd come here and bring me flowers, open the door, just the whole nine yards, waited on me hand and foot. He would even have wiped my mouth if I wanted him to.

"He was very romantic too. I had a good time with him, but,

like I said, he's very, very busy with his business. You know what I mean.

"Some black men, when you go out with them, they want you to pay half. Yeah, yeah, sometimes they want you to pay both. They don't usually open the door for you unless they're trying to impress you. That's the way Greg was.

"I was more in love with him because I could relate to him better. We were more familiar to each other. For example, we could argue with each other, and Bill and I couldn't.

"Isn't that sick? I was more in love with the one I could argue with, the one who did not treat me best, the one who was always trying to borrow money from me or get me to pay for something that Bill would have gladly paid for.

"One thing, though. Greg was a fantasy guy. He's six feet five inches, two hundred forty pounds. He can pick me up. My husband couldn't pick me up. I was as big as he was. I'm a hundred fifty-five pounds. I got big hips.

"I went for Greg the minute he walked through the door. He has this gorgeous complexion. He's a little lighter than me. I would call him brown skin like a Dominican. He's not yellow; he's about a shade lighter than me. He has Indian in his family. So he has a very, very gorgeous complexion. Hair on the chest, which I like, and he looks good in jeans, suits, and shorts. What can I say? He's a piece of work, bottom line. Okay.

"He had a nice personality, but he was a manipulator. But he could never manipulate me and this is why we fought. Women were all over him. He's very spoiled. So with me he met his match, and we fought all the time, and there was friction. He wants things his way, and if I feel it's not correct, you're not getting it.

"And also, I had to definitely not let him run over me, because then he wouldn't have respected me and he always said he didn't need another dog. I don't think he respected women. He said he didn't want another dog, but then he would try to treat a woman like his dog.

"To tell you the truth, I don't think he could handle me. He was very insecure. He's always doing something to prove himself. I like a man who doesn't always need reassurance. He always needed reassurance. I didn't want to be his cheerleader.

"You know. The bottom line is I don't have time for the foolishness. I'm about being progressive. I want a guy like that too. You know what I mean? I don't want someone who needs me to say he's all right. It's the cocaine. He wants me to tell him he's all right when he's into his coke and I don't think he's all right.

"One time he might be very cocky and sure of himself. He was very aggressive, but the next time he might've wanted me to be tender and understanding, and pick up on some remark that he said, and then he'd want to blame me for not being sensitive to this thing he said, and I didn't even know how important it was.

"And so he'd want me to be sympathetic, but I never knew when the other personality was gonna come back, and he would be trying to kick my ass. He might fake you into being sympathetic, and then all of a sudden he becomes the ass kicker and you're a in soft mood.

"That coke made him act crazy. Like I said, he made good money, lives in a nice town house over near the University of Illinois, Chicago Circle campus. But all of his money goes toward coke, and he was getting so out of control. He was starting to imagine things, like something was crawling all over his body, but still he kept smoking that pipe. He was on crack.

"I couldn't be in love with him, because I couldn't get caught in that. We couldn't even talk about his profession or my profession. Because the mind was somewhere else, most of the time. Most of the time we couldn't talk about anything that made sense, because the mind jumped around. You sit there and different per-

sonalities come up, and you don't know who the fuck you're dealing with. But I was hooked on him. I could say I loved him.

"He has a good job. He has a master's degree in computer
science. He's a networking consultant for a computer consulting
company. I just felt, with his background and his knowledge . . .
because when he's not high he's smart, and I just saw the potential,
and I just thought the two of us, based on what I do and what he
does . . . and the attraction, it was cool.

"We could have done more with our lives. We were good
together in terms of partying, we had good times. He was one
man who I didn't have to have anything to drink to get excited
over him. I was excited by his presence. It was the chemistry,
that's all.

"I was totally comfortable with him. I can't explain it. It was
that chemistry and it was the mix, but I always had to be on my
guard against that Jekyll-and-Hyde personality.

"And you know what else turns me off: him using up all his
money and borrowing money from me, calling me up and saying,
'Baby, can I borrow fifty dollars and I'll give it back to you on
Monday?'

"Here's a guy who makes seventy thousand dollars a year and
he's borrowing fifty dollars. I didn't want that. I didn't want that,
because that was just pulling me down. So we fought all the time.
'I don't care if you're high or not. If you say something that's
incorrect, I'm going to call you on it, bottom line, high or not,' I
told him.

"So the last time we had a fight that went on for weeks. Not
a physical fight. He wouldn't hit a woman. I mean a vicious argument.

"It started when I had given him forty dollars. He called me
from work and said he had to come by to borrow forty dollars. I
gave him forty dollars and gave him a bottle of vodka, and I told
him, 'If you get in trouble tonight, call me, but I'm giving you

this bottle of vodka, so you won't have go over to the bar.' Because I knew he was going to use the forty dollars to buy crack.

"And sure enough, at eleven o'clock he called me. I went over to his house and he was completely drunk, and he had taken the money and bought coke and was definitely gone. I stayed over there because he was crying and shit.

"And in the morning when I was getting ready to leave he said, 'Are you giving me seven dollars to take a cab to work?' So I said, 'I just gave you forty dollars last night.'

"He said, 'Baby, I don't have any money, you saw me screw it up. You didn't do anything to stop me, and you didn't do it with me.' He was in a rage. He said: 'You know what, when I give you that forty dollars back today, I'm not seeing you anymore. I'm not dealing with you anymore.'

"I said, 'Good, the feeling is mutual. I don't need a liability and I don't need an asshole.' And I slammed his door. And later on, at twelve, the personality has switched, okay, and he called me at work and said, 'Baby, sweetheart, I just wanted you to know the money is in the bank and I'm going to leave the money with the doorman.' Because that's what I told him to do: 'Leave it downstairs, because I don't need to see your sorry ass.'

"But, like I said, this argument went on for weeks. I wanted my goddamn forty dollars. It wasn't the forty dollars. I just wanted him to give me my money. And he kept begging me to be sympathetic, because he didn't want to give me the forty dollars, because he wanted to start a pattern of using my money for his habit.

"And he knew if he gave me my forty dollars, I might make good on his threat to break off the relationship. Then one night he said he wanted to come over and talk. I wanted him to come over and talk because I was going to tie into his ass. I wanted him to know that we could have made it if he was half the man he could have been.

"I told him not to bring his shit here to begin with that night.

Okay, he didn't listen to what I said. This was when my father was in the hospital before he died, and he said he was coming over to console me, or whatever the case may be, and he brought a fifth of vodka, and some crack and his pipe. He spent the night with me, bottom line.

"I put him out at seven because I was tired of his ass. When you're on that stuff you can't sleep and he had kept me up all night. As soon as he got to his house, he called me, and he said, 'Baby, I think I have a heart problem,' and I said, 'Go to work.'

"He said, 'Baby, I'm not going to work.' And then he called me at about ten and said, 'I changed my mind. I'm at work, and when I get off work I'm coming back over.' I told him not to come. He must have called me at least six times that day, Friday.

"Finally I said, 'Fine, but don't bring any drugs over.' He said, 'Okay.' So I went shopping, bought food so we could eat. And he called me at nine P.M. and said, 'I bought you a bottle of Absolut. No drugs, just a little vodka.'

"When he got here, I said, 'You know, tomorrow, I have to go to the hospital, my father is in the hospital, and I really need to get some sleep,' and he started doing that coke, and it just got on my nerves, and I couldn't deal with it anymore.

"He was just not good company. He really ticked me off, and he laid on my sofa and I thought he was going to burn it and it was leather. So I took my cigarette and burned his ass. I lost control and I wasn't going to let him do that. I had a lot of family problems. I just had too much shit in my head to be aggravated by anyone. He got up and sort of smacked me, because I burned him. He never smacked me before. I fell.

"He didn't knock me down. I fell. I could have fought him. I'm strong, but I wasn't going to tear my place up. I got up, went downstairs, and told the doorman to send the police. And they came. The police came in two minutes.

"I said: 'I think my friend had too much to drink and I just want him to go home.' I didn't have him arrested. They didn't handcuff him or anything. They didn't find the pipe. I didn't tell them about the crack. I didn't want that on me.

"But afterward he still talked about me anyway. He said that black women are too hard. They are not sympathetic. They are too tough. They are selfish. He poured it on. He said he had gotten into a program and that I should give him another chance.

"But I thought it was all a game. The reason he went into the program is because he knew that I had enough shit and I wasn't going to deal with him anymore, and I told him I didn't need the money he owed me, and I didn't even want it.

" 'Just keep going, because I don't want you to have a reason to come here. I don't want to deal with you and I don't see any reason why we should deal with each other on any level. I don't even want to be your friend.'

"So he went into a program, but by this time I was cured of him and cured of love in a way. I mean, I liked the way Bill treated me, but I don't think I could be with a white man totally, in America as it is.

"And with me and black men, it's over as far as I'm concerned. I wouldn't find a man like my husband very exciting. He's a good guy, don't get me wrong, but I wouldn't find him exciting, and here Greg was, a man who could get me excited almost enough to climax sexually just by being with me, and he couldn't even manage that.

"All he could manage was all that oral sex shit. All of that oral shit is okay, but it's like you bought me the icing and didn't bring the cake. Bottom line. I need to be fucked. In order for me to be happy, someone needs to really fuck me.

"You tell someone what you need and they keep not hearing you. They keep giving you what they say you need, which just happens to be the only thing they're equipped to give after they've had all of that coke. 'Baby, this is what you need,' they say, and sit there smoking their crack pipe.

"I say, 'Baby, I just told you what I need. I need someone to fuck me.' I didn't tell Greg that, but my husband fucked me. He fucked me good. Bottom line. Okay?"

Love's GONNA GET YA

"When you have a couple of teenagers in love, and a million dollars involved, then things can get very complicated," Candi said.

"Two and a half million," I said.

"Is that what he gets paid?"

"Two and a half million dollars a year." I had read that figure in the papers.

"More power to him. I'm happy for him, because everybody involved in the entire thing was both right and wrong—the newspapers, the police, him, me, the people in the university who wanted him expelled, the people who defended him. The women who wanted me to press charges against him for rape.

"The professors who tried to band together and say that none of them would allow him in their shitty little classes, so in that way he couldn't stay in school. The people who tried to organize a boycott against the basketball team.

"No one knew the whole story and he and I couldn't tell the whole story. My father was wrong, my mother was wrong, and yet from their points of view, based on what they knew, they were right," Candi said. She was lounging on the sofa in her apartment. She was a tall young woman, with jet black hair combed into a feathery effect. She had beautiful white teeth and huge eyes.

I said: "I'm sad because I wish you two were together. I see him on TV now and I think about you and I think that he needs you, especially with all that money, he needs you."

"I loved him, but not because of the money. We had the fairy-tale love affair before the money. I loved him because he was just wonderful. I guess I loved him because of the way he made me feel. I felt very special. Men have always made me feel special, but he made me feel like I was the only woman alive. He focused all of his attention on me. It was all about me—what made me happy, what I wanted.''

"Do you think you two might get back together?''

"There's a court order that he can't even call me. And anyway, I don't think I would want to get back with him. It wouldn't be the same.''

"How did you meet?'' I asked. I knew some of the details from the newspaper clips I had read.

"I was attending St. Francis College, about twelve miles from the university [where he was an all-conference basketball player in his freshman year].

"I was on a date with a guy from the university and I got mad at him because he was an asshole and so I left him. I didn't know anybody at the university, but I'm in Delta Sigma Theta Sorority and he's in Omega Psi Phi Fraternity, and we're like sister and brother.

"At that time of night there were no buses and that town didn't have good taxi service, so I went to the security guard and told him to go in the dormitory and find a member of Omega Psi Phi to come down and drive me home.

"And there he was. When he came down he was so-o-o hot. Yeah, he was hot. Tall, built, light brown eyes. He was just gorgeous.

"I was turned on to him the first time I saw him. You know when you first see somebody and you get that feeling. My blood started running hot in my veins, and I got excited and was on my way to going crazy, just from being in the car with him. He had that effect on me.

"We made love the first night and it was unlike anything I ever experienced. I'm an island girl. I was born in Jamaica. Hot-blooded, so, 'Come on.' 'Come on.' He was in shape. I was in shape. We wore each other out.

"It moved really, really fast. We got intense so quickly. Soon we were always together. I was not in love with him because I was looking forward to him making all this money in pro basketball. Our relationship was not about that. It was mostly about me. I felt like if I was alone with him on a secluded island that would be enough.

"He had that power in himself and I think the basketball thing was just an expression of that power he had in himself and I felt wonderful when I felt all that power directed toward me. He was all I needed. He was my everything.

"He almost came to live in my dormitory room. He was over there so much. My roommate actually moved out and so I had the room to myself and he was there all the time. If we were apart we were on the phone," she said.

"What did he love about you?" I asked.

"He thought I was unique. I was different than anybody he had met before. I was sweet, attractive, tall, funny. He loved me. Everything. The silly things that I do.

"I could look in his eyes and know how much he loved me without him saying the words. The way he looked at me. He would look at me sometimes and I would feel like I'm melting.

"He made me really happy. I always had this smile on my face. When I was with him I felt that there was nothing I couldn't do. I could do it all. I felt like I owned the world. Everybody could tell. I was glowing, and there was an extra kick in my stride.

"Being with him made me rise to my full potential as a woman—I was like those women that you read about in a book and you say I wish I would meet somebody like that, that's the way I was. I was sweet. I was fun. I was nice to be with. I was crazy. I was wild. I could have a discussion about any topic. I could be like a child. I could be whatever.

"Everything was so positive in my life when I was with him. I saw no faults in him. That's why I call it my fairy-tale love. I had had loves before, but I learned that I only thought I was in love.

"I justified everything by the fact that I loved him. I felt that there was nothing I would not have done for him. I washed his clothes for him. I used to love to wear his clothes. Sometimes he'd leave something in my room, and I would just pick it up and put it on and wear it all day. I used to like to leave his clothes in my bed. I would sleep with his clothes.

"So it wasn't about his going into pro basketball and making a lot of money. It's not that we didn't talk about basketball. I used to watch the games with him, but basketball was not the center of our relationship.

"In fact, he stayed over on my campus in my dorm so he could get away from the people at the university who always forced him to think about basketball.

"But when we did watch basketball, he liked the fact that I knew a lot about it, and had loved it even before I met him. He had had problems with that before, women not knowing anything, or caring anything, about sports and him planning to make his living in sports.

"We could hang out on weekends and watch sports and argue about sports, and this wasn't faking arguments just to make him happy. I had strong opinions about the Portland Trailblazers, and of course he liked the Chicago Bulls.

"I was in heaven. I was his buddy. I was his babee. I was his friend. I was his lover, whatever I needed to be. I mean, we were such big buddies that we would actually get into a scuffle over a basketball game on television. I was all the way in it with him.

"It was a very physical relationship. The thing we liked most was making love. We liked each other's bodies and so we used to spend a lot of time in the room with no clothes on, but not making love. I used to have him lay his head on my lap and I would wash his hair.

"We thought about the money, but he was not dreaming about making all this money. He knew that it didn't take much to make me happy. He knew he could just write on a piece of paper that he was thinking of me, and mail that to me, and that would make me happy. He used to do that all the time.

"Or just leave me a message on my answering machine that 'I think you're really terrific,' and he knew I would come home and that would put a big smile on my face until he finally got here.

"More than anything he talked about the money as a means of making me happier. He was going to own the world and he was going to give it to me. He said he would get joy out of watching me enjoy. He was not lying about this. That's the kind of person he was. This was so unlike anything I had ever experienced.

"As I said, the thing that attracted me most was that he was always worrying about what would make me happy. It was like he forgot his own self, and every time he saw me he always had a surprise for me—a poem, a letter—nothing that cost money because he didn't have money. He did it all. He stripped for me. He was childish like me. He could be really silly too. We were like two little kids having fun.

"We used to have peanut-butter-and-jelly candlelight dinners. Whatever we had was all right. We had it. With some music in the background. We were in heaven. We had holidays every day.

"I always had a way to make things big, much bigger than what they were, and he loved that. He used to listen to me sing. I can't sing. That's why he was special. He actually listened."

She got up and began looking around the apartment for something. She found it in a sideboard drawer and brought it back and sat again on the sofa.

"He'd say, 'You sound so good, baby.' He didn't sing, and couldn't dance. He has no rhythm. No rhythm. In public I could only dance slow songs with him.

"He used to write poems to me even though he wasn't a poet. His poems were sweet." She began reading:

Since the first time I saw you
I knew you were a queen.
Ever since the first day
my life has been like a dream.
The first day you turned my
world upside down.
A couple of months later
I still haven't hit the
ground.
My love for you grows
with each passing day.
I cannot believe
you make me feel this way.

"No, he's not a poet," I said.

"You should hear my singing," she said. "We just loved each other. It didn't matter. When I first met him I was totally against getting married. I never wanted to hear the word *marriage.* If I ever got married I would want it to be forever, until death do us part, that was the way I wanted it.

"And I know that that's impossible, in the world today. I saw my parents after twenty-some years of marriage decide to get a divorce.

"I stopped believing in the institution. It's just getting up there in front of the preacher and lying and saying I'm going to be with this person in sickness and in health. I don't know that I want to make that kind of commitment.

"Yet I knew that if I did get married I wanted it to last. I felt that divorce was just an easy way out, so I told myself that I never wanted to get married. I was completely against it. There are a lot of people my age who don't believe in marriage because of what we saw our parents go through," she said.

I remembered the group interview that I had done with thirty high school kids out at Ball State University in Indiana. I was surprised at how many of them had never seen a happy marriage, ever.

I remember one girl of about sixteen who said she was going to get married, have her baby, and then dump the guy, because she didn't want her baby born out of wedlock but she didn't want to be married either. She didn't trust marriage.

Candi was agreeing with these youngsters. "I was afraid to death of marriage because, as I said, at a very young age I was caught in the middle of a knock-down, drag-out, police-calling, ugly-for-years divorce.

"He talked about marriage, and I knew he wanted to be with me. And we would go to places and he would see little kids playing and he would talk about our kids playing like that. I started to believe in it because I felt like he was different. I had found my soul mate and we were going to be together forever. Everything was right.

"We fit so well that I started to imagine that we could be together until death do us part. And he told me every day that we would be together. He was sincere. He wasn't jive. He wasn't jive at all.

"What people don't know is that he was a very honest person. He had been in trouble back in Brooklyn, but he was still a very honest person. He was always honest with himself, and he was honest with me.

"We didn't go to church, but we both believed that there was a higher being, someone you had to answer to, and therefore you had to live your life in a certain way—trying to do what was right.

"The thing that happened in Brooklyn was just one of those things that happen to black males in this society, especially big ones who assert their rights.

"He was really a guy who was very respectful of other people's feelings. He was always looking out for the way the other person might feel. Because he was so big, he could actually back down from things without feeling like a coward, and he did.

"There were ways for a college superstar to get money illegally. It's done all the time, but he wouldn't do it. Toward the end it seemed that he was the kind who was taking money illegally for agents, but that wasn't true. He just needed money in the end to pay lawyers to get him out of the trouble.

"But during the time I was with him he was broke all the time. He would have to call his parents to get money so he could come across town to see me and be with me. Twenty, thirty, forty dollars—amounts that small. That's what he was living on, you know.

"What the newspapers didn't report because they didn't know and we couldn't tell them is that I broke up with him because I thought I was pregnant, and for the first time all the money that he was going to make in the NBA became an issue.

"First of all, he wanted to quit school and get married. He wanted to quit school, not go into the NBA, but get a job. I didn't want him to do that. I couldn't marry him when I knew what he would give up. He hadn't made a good enough reputation to quit college early and apply for early entry to the NBA.

"He was talking crazy. It was almost like a relief to him. For the first time since he was five years old he didn't have basketball hanging over him, he said.

"Since he was in junior high school everyone he knew had been looking forward to him playing pro ball. His father was a great basketball player who had never had the chance to play in the pros, but it hadn't been as easy back in his father's day for black guys to get into the right colleges to get positioned to go into the pros.

"It seemed like he *wanted* to quit school. It looked like he was having a lapse that he would regret later, that he might regret after it was too late, and then he would look at me and the baby as the reason why he didn't complete his plans. I didn't want him to give that up.

"I didn't want our marriage to be a temporary lapse on the way to wherever it was that he was supposed to go," she said.

"But you didn't mind letting love be that."

"Maybe that's what love really should be. Maybe then there wouldn't be so many divorces after you've gotten up and promised until death do us part, and all that crap," she said bitterly.

"No, I was agreeing with you," I said.

"It was like his love for me was the thing that would not allow him to be himself. I have that effect on men. Yet I knew that Tony had to go on and be himself, and I didn't want his love for me to prevent it.

"It was really intense. He started buying clothes for the baby. He started looking for jobs. So I quit him. It was the most painful decision I had to make, but I loved him enough to make that decision, and I would have done whatever it took to break off the relationship.

"I think that when you have love you have to learn how to compromise. That's what I did wrong. I didn't compromise. I've always been a person who wants what she wants when she wants it, no compromise.

"I started feeling that I was right and I didn't want to see that the other person could be right also. Also, I didn't want to marry him and have it seem that I just got pregnant so that I could marry him because he was going to make all that money. I didn't want it to be a case of him being forced to marry me, or him ever thinking that I had trapped him into marriage with the baby.

"I thought that we'd never be able to sit down and watch a basketball game without him thinking about what could have been if he had been able to finish his last two years of college and been drafted.

"He didn't want to accept it. I wouldn't talk to him because I felt I was doing the right thing. I felt noble. So I went to the courts and got an order of protection so he couldn't come on campus. By this time I was a little afraid of him.

"Then one night he came on campus and kicked my door in, and I had to go with him so the police wouldn't come get him because the local police might have shot him because they would have been afraid of a black man so big.

"So I went with him and that's where the kidnapping story came from. He had borrowed a car from his roommate, but when the police went looking for him because someone told them about the door he kicked in, his roommate didn't tell the police that he had loaned Tony the car.

"So his roommate was up on charges of aiding and abetting in the kidnap charges. He was heading back to New York. We stopped at a motel and we argued, and we had always been very physical in lovemaking.

"A lot of times I teased him and forced him to wrestle with me, and so this is what happened, but this time I didn't want him to have me because I was afraid that if he did I would not be able to continue breaking it off. I couldn't scream because I didn't want to call the police into it.

"So I fought back as hard as I could. I'm very strong. I dug my fingernails into his skin and he hit me. That's how I got the bruise on my face that the police found. That's where the rape charges came from. They found us by tracing the roommate's car.

"The police were especially interested in making a case against Tony, especially with so much news about spousal abuse. Violence against women.

"The police have to treat rape cases like this, and he being a black guy from Brooklyn, who was going to make all this money in the NBA. There was a lot of jealousy involved, on top of the justifiable seriousness that police ought to have on all cases like this.

"And the newspapers, they do things like that, publish unfounded statements by women's organizations that an NBA agent, or the university, or rich alumni, had paid me off not to press charges. No such thing happened. I didn't press charges because there was more to the story than the police or the newspapers knew.

"I had often fought Tony back when we made love. He was so big that I could fight him back with all my might, and I enjoyed that, but this time I didn't want to be subdued because I knew that if we made love I might give in in the area of marriage also and that would lead to divorce, as it always does.

"The police wanted to think the worst anyway. We couldn't tell anyone about me thinking I was pregnant. Then I found out that I wasn't pregnant. We had both panicked. Or else, I don't know. I had never gone to the doctor. Maybe in all of the excitement, I was pregnant and the excitement brought my period on. I don't know," she said.

I said: "I hope you two get back together. Stop thinking of your sake. He might need you. You know that Magic Johnson went back and married his former sweetheart."

"I don't know. It's not like I don't have some plans of my own," she said.

"I heard that," I said. "Yeah, okay."

"He used to call me, but I wouldn't talk to him. He ignored the court order and called because he knew I won't turn him in because there's more to it than him being guilty," she said.

"Maybe he'll ignore the court order and come back to see you."

"I don't think I want to start it up again."

"You think you lost the feeling?"

"I don't know and I don't want to find out.

"When you have a memory like that. I don't want to go back with him and if anything was different, I'd be disappointed. And even if we got back together, what guarantee do you have? This way you have the guarantee that you've had this fairy-tale love.

"If we got back together, I'd be looking for anything that was different and I wouldn't get married because I'd really be afraid of divorce. I mean, isn't that the way it always ends? Nobody has to be at fault. Something always happens like it happened to us."

"And sometimes the more money that's involved, the uglier it can get," I said.

"The only way you can be sure is to make yourself happy with the amount of money you yourself can earn, not somebody else's money," she said.

Love DON'T NEED

NO REASONS

*J*ames Mayo made the obvious statement "Indiana is different than New York. We do most things a little different out here in Muncie," he said.

"What's the big difference as far as love is concerned?" I asked.

"This is the Bible Belt—not really the Bible Belt. You usually think of Oklahoma, down in there, as the Bible Belt, but out here it's very similar except that there are many fewer black folk in the rural areas, but there is a KKK town just down the road from Muncie. Black folk don't go in that town.

"On the other hand, I was raised out in the country, and what's true about our family is true about the white farm families in the area."

"About love?"

"About love. Of course, each person's experience is unique, and yet there are some basic similarities and these carry across racial lines."

"Basic similarities between love here and love in New York?" I asked, just to provoke him.

He smiled to concede.

I told him about an interview that I had conducted with about thirty high school–age kids who were at a workshop over on the Ball State University campus. One of the high school girls had said proudly: "I'm a user. If a man is stupid enough to be used, then I *will* use him."

It was a bolder statement than I had gotten from the interview I had done in the New York area with a group of college-age youngsters in Newark.

I had been surprised. James Mayo was surprised. We were in his apartment not far from the campus of Ball State. Earlier he had told me: "The relationship that I had just before I got married to Cora, my wife, was the relationship that taught me the most about love. It was a very painful relationship." He said this in a slow, solemn voice that made it seem like he was reciting a pledge.

I was trying to make the point that this kind of relationship could have happened anywhere in America. We had talked about love in the Western world, about the blues and love, about gospel and love, and about love in the Eastern cities, in California, and in the rural areas of the Midwest, where he had spent his entire life.

Earlier he had said: "I don't know why it seems we are attached to our pain, but I was attached to this relationship for five years and it was the one that taught me most, through pain. But in hindsight there were things in it that I should have known that I didn't want to know."

I thought about what Denis de Rougemont had written in *Love in the Western World* that love is always associated with pain, and the greater the love, the greater the pain; and that in a person's life there is one great monumental love that ends tragically, and the person spends the rest of his or her life yearning either openly or secretly for that one great, lost love.

In order to see if this was true in James Mayo's case, I concluded that I would listen closely to whatever he had to say about the love he had had before he met and married his wife.

James Mayo had agreed with part of de Rougemont's statement. When I brought the statement up he knew that I was tactfully asking about that one big relationship he had had.

"I'm over the hurt. I'm over the hurt. I'm over the hurt," he said. I was sorry that I had put him on the defensive. I knew that it is impossible to prove a negative. He could not prove that he was not still in love with Hildah Ali. At some point I would simply have to believe or not believe.

"If she walked in this door right now, I'd be just as kind and loving, but I'm not in love with her anymore. I still don't want her to be unhappy. I want her to be happy right now. I'm over it in terms of being in love with her. I wish her well.

"I hope she has resources to do whatever she wants to do in life. I hope she is laughing and having a good time right now. I don't want her to be unhappy, but I know how life is. Life doesn't give us those things all the time.

"You and I are going to go through a certain amount of pain. That's part of the human dilemma. There's nothing we can do about that.

"We're put here on this earth in human form and so we're going to experience both good and bad things. It's how we respond to those things that determines whether or not we are happy.

"We had our time, Hildah and I. We were together for five years. We were close. We were very, very close.

"My philosophy is that I am walking through the earth, and at some time I will come to the end of my physical journey here, and part of the thing that is helping me to reach a higher spiritual level is going trough a sequence of experiences, good and painful. How can you know the good if you haven't experienced the bad? How can you know? I used to always say, 'I want a good woman,' 'I want a good woman.' Well, would I know her if I had her? Would I really know?

"The only way we can really know if we got a good woman is that, Lord God, you got to have some experiences, but I'm not saying by that that Hildah was a bad woman.

"Every decade I had one or two enduring relationships, and

each one got better. I've known several women in my life, I mean several women," he said, but at this point in the interview I believed that none of these women affected him like Hildah.

"I know that I was in love with her because she taught me the difference between loving and being in love," he said.

I decided not to ask him the difference. While interviewing other people I had more often heard that being in love was superior to loving. Someone might say, 'I love John Doe, but I'm not in love with John Doe.' He was saying the opposite, that loving was a superior state to being in love.

"I'm now very glad that I didn't marry Hildah, because although I would have been in love, in fact, I was in love, but I would never have realized my potential as a loving person," he said, leaning forward and putting a tone of hushed urgency in his voice.

His voice seemed to asked if I understood. I didn't, but I knew that his story would somehow tell me better than he could explain it to me.

"It probably never would have worked out because we were unequally yoked from a spiritual perspective. I honestly believe that for a happy marital relationship both people have to have the same spiritual connection," he said, as if this were the explanation that would make it clear to me.

It didn't.

"They have to want the same thing spiritually, and this is important not only in the good times but especially in the bad times. What do they want to do in life? And how do they want to go about doing it?"

"Is religion a consolation and escape after you lost the love?"

"No. No. I've been religious all my life," he said in that same hushed, urgent voice. "Mother and Daddy raised us that way. My father and mother had one of the neatest relationships, and I guess I took some of that from them.

"I know that he and my mother had this relationship, this very close relationship. I never heard my father raise his voice to my mother. Never.

"He was a very gentle man. She was like a drill sergeant. I'm more like my father," he said in an even more hushed voice.

"Have you looked for women to love who are like your mother?" I asked.

"With some of the same qualities, yes, but I've never found anyone like her. I'm from a farm family. I'm very proud of that heritage. I was one of twelve children. I never knew that I was poor until I was a freshman in college.

"The money may not have been in abundance, but we were eating and we had clean clothing. Mother and Daddy had a very long, enduring marriage. Prior to his death they had been married forty-eight years, and one day prior to his death I asked my father, 'Daddy, how did you and Mother make it all these years?'

"He said, 'Well, son, we have a oneness in God, *in* God.' That didn't make sense as a full answer then, but I never forgot it."

About Hildah, I wanted to ask him if he thought that she might just have wanted to get someone to help her through college. I heard echoes of the teenager who had said: "I'm a user. If a man is stupid enough to be used, then I *will* use him."

But before I could ask him he said: "I believe in my heart, to this day, that Hildah is a good person, that she is a very loving person. In my heart I think she's a real decent person. I always will. I think she had a very big heart. I just think that she had to find a way to do it and this is how she did it."

"Okay, but still, it could mean that with Hildah you took your excursion out in the world and then, when it didn't work, you moved back to the most familiar consolation you knew, religion."

"Okay. Maybe that's what learning is, coming back to the truth you've always known. I've learned. I haven't always been this way.

It has been a very painful process for me, and I don't mean to say that I have arrived either, but I'm still learning," he said.

Earlier he had told me the story of the love that he and I had agreed was the one big love of his life, prior to meeting his wife: "Hildah was a student here at the university," he had said. "She had come out here from Cleveland to get her degree. I met her when I was making deliveries up at the university. My family owns a business that supplies local produce, fruits and vegetables and such, to the university dining halls.

"My father had died, and so me and my brothers took over the business. They stayed out on the farm and I worked mostly in Muncie, lining up restaurants, stores, and institutions to sell our products to. By that I mean that home is out in the country, on the farm, but I have an apartment in the city.

"I was up at the dining hall at the university and I saw this woman, it was Hildah, and she was eating alone, and I kept looking at her and she kept looking at me, and I smiled at her and she smiled at me.

"We started talking, and so on and so forth, but I knew I was already in love with her. I do believe in love at first sight. It's not the sight, the visual part of it; it's the feeling that passes between you.

"I knew that I was in love with this woman. All I had to do was wait while everything fell into place, as I knew it would.

"I took her out to the farm, and my brothers and sisters liked her. She liked being out there, and even though she was from Cleveland, she pitched right in with the livestock and the farming. She loved it. I know she loved it. You can't fake things like that. She loved it.

"My family always believed in marriage, but this was a relationship that was very different than what we were used to, and they all knew how happy this woman made me, and so she moved into the apartment I kept in the city without us being married.

"I don't know until this day if one of the reasons why it didn't work out was that I had violated the laws of God by living with a woman without being married. But it was just like we were married, just without the license.

"I was in love with her, but in my dream . . . at least I thought we both were dreaming that she would finish her education, we would get married, we'd buy a little house or maybe build a little house, and have a couple of crumb snatchers running around. We used to talk about this, but in hindsight I was the one talking about it. She just sat and listened. To this day I wonder what she was really thinking while I was talking and she was silent.

"I don't think she was scheming. I don't think that. I spent a lot of money trying to help her get through school. It was devastating. I gave her everything I could give her. She finished her degree and she left and I haven't seen her since. She left. She left. I came home one day and all of her things were gone, and I haven't seen her since."

I wondered if he really wanted to know why she left. Should he really want to know?

He continued: "To this day she still hasn't given me any reason why she left. Even though I'm happily married to my wife, and I love my wife very dearly, I'd like to know.

"It didn't sour me on life because I think that my religious faith is the foundation that kept me going. I searched my soul and said: 'What did I do? What did I do? Or what did she perceive that I had done, or didn't do?' I wanted to know, honestly.

"I was depressed. I reached a level of despair that I never knew. Once she left, I was trying to date again, and no woman gave me pleasure. There was just so much pain. Death remembers me. Death and I became very close friends. My heart was really, really hurting.

"I just wanted to sit and talk with her—not being judgmental, not being a persecutor. I just wanted to ask, 'I really want to know why you left.' Even if she was going to leave, I wish that she had left me a note: 'You dirty rascal, I'm leaving you.'

"But she didn't. I came home, she was gone. Then, in hindsight, there were cues that something was in the air. She would say that she loved me, but her behavior didn't seem to say that. As I remember correctly, she made love but she never said very much about being in love.

"There were times when I suspected that she was unhappy because I always felt that this town was too slow for her. She was used to a big city. I don't hold anything against her.

"I do feel that there was probably another man in the picture. Probably the man she's married to now," he said.

About her behavior, I thought of a song by Smokey Robinson: "Love Don't Need No Reasons." About his behavior, I thought that the song should be "Love Don't Know No Reasons." Or was it "Love Don't Want No Reasons," which goes back to "Love Don't Need No Reasons" in his case too? Does it ever? Should it?

He said: "I need to bring closure to this. I want closure, but I really believe that one day I will see her again. My wife and I have talked about this. My wife knows.

"My wife knows that this woman was very, very important to me. If Hildah walked through that door of our house right now, I would be just as loving. My wife would not feel threatened. I would say: 'Hildah, this is my wife, Cora. Cora, this is Hildah.'

"I do now know that Hildah is married. She has a child. I could hold her child. I can now hold her baby and love her and her baby, but that's only because I now have my wife," he said, and deepened the urgency in his voice.

"How did you meet your wife?" I asked.

"Just after Hildah left, one night I was lying in bed, and, as I said, I had reached this level of despair that I never ever knew. I was so sad. I felt that my heart was literally going to burst out of my body. I felt so alone.

"I felt that I was literally going to die. And this was early one morning, about three A.M. one morning. So I prayed to God. I said to God: 'You know, I want You to send me someone to love, and I want her to be really into the Word, so we can both be equally yoked.' "

As he spoke I thought of the lines of an old blues song that I had first heard sung by Percy Mayfield. It was actually a prayer that God send him someone to love, that God sends us all someone to love.

As James and I had said before, the blues tradition is a more recent modification of the love in the Western world tradition that he and I had talked about. The blues tradition said that you can come through the suffering and love again and again and again, but that is not what had happened to him.

He continued: "Three days later I went to the movies. And before the movie started, I was sitting there and in walked this woman with an elderly woman. I had never in my life seen a woman like this. I said, 'My God. It's her.'

"And one thing that really turned me on too was she was with an elderly woman, and I said, 'This woman loves elderly people.' And I have this thing too about elderly folk, because I remember that before my mother died, I had a chance to hold her in my arms and pull her to me, and that was the greatest feeling of love I had ever had.

"I said, 'Who is this woman?' I have never . . . even the older woman. It was like these women dropped out of space. My wife tells me now that her perception of me was that I was just sitting there grinning.

"I had never in my life seen such a woman. It wasn't the physical stuff. It was something else. It was something else. I said: 'My God, this has got to be the woman. This is her. This is nice. This is nice. I started seeing myself with her, hand-in-hand, and nothing physical or sexual came in the picture.

"Because it wasn't like I was just sexually attracted to her, naw, it was something else. 'Aw, man, aw, man.' So after the movie was over we were walking out. We began walking and talking together and she said: 'My name is Cora Kinard and this is my grandmother, Mammie Prichard.' I said, 'Hi, I'm James Mayo.'

"I asked: 'Do you come here often?'

"She said 'No. Do you?'

"I said, 'No, I just work in the area. I'm one of the suppliers to the university. I supply fruits and vegetables to the university dining halls.'

"Well, anyway, I went to my car and she went to her car and we drove off and then I realized that I had forgotten the woman's name, I was so excited. I had forgotten her name.

"I was sure I had blew everything, so anyway, I was in my office a few days later and the telephone rang. I usually let my secretary pick up the phone. I very seldom pick up the phone, but for some reason that day I picked up the phone and a voice said: 'Hi, I'm Cora Kinard.'

'It's her,' I said. 'God, it's her.'

"She said: 'I don't get in a habit of calling men, but my grandmother and I were talking and she said that you seemed very nice. I remembered that you said you supplied produce to the university, and so I called the university and they gave me the number of your business.'

"I said to myself: 'I'm gonna act on this.' So I said, 'What are you doing this evening?'

" 'I got to run some errands for Grandmama,' she said. 'Then I'm free.'

" 'Would you meet me at Oliver's for a bite to eat?'

"She said, 'Yes.'

"I got to Oliver's early and I was sitting up there on a stool at the bar. I don't drink but I waited at the bar. I was sitting there and my heart was just pounding. I had an image of her in my mind.

"Then I saw her. She had on a white outfit, and I could have died. This woman walked in there and I just fell in love with her again from the first meeting. I was sharp. I felt good and I knew I looked good. I felt that I had it all together that night.

"I had met my soul mate. I had met her. When we were walking together back to the table for dinner, I said: 'She's mine.' That's what I said to myself: 'This is her. Without a shadow of a doubt. This is her. God, you've answered my prayers.'

"That night we got along so well, and the next night, and I kept seeing her. Gradually I learned that she is a caregiver for her grandmother and her uncle. She spends a lot of time taking them to get their groceries, taking them to buy their medication.

"She has a bachelor's degree from the university and she wants to be a counselor. I learned that she had loads of friends and they were always calling her for advice. She's a caregiver.

"I saw her almost every night for about a year and we got married and we haven't had an argument. Her grandmother and uncle live in this house that we own. I baby her a lot.

"I love what we have now and I'm trying to treat it with the utmost respect. I think I've really learned how to love a woman. I think I've really learned how to love myself.

"Here is a man who has learned and seasoned and matured over time. It runs real, real deep. I'm the kind of man who likes to get with one woman and stays. I don't like being like a doorknob that everybody gets to turn. I don't like that. That's too crazy.

"But the most important thing is we both have this very deep abiding love for Christ in our lives. That's part of who we are, and I'm not saying we're Mr. and Mrs. Goody Two-shoes. I'm not talking about that. I'm just saying that we got this close relationship to God.

"It's a pleasure going home. I can't wait to see her. I'm going home right now. It's fantastic," he said.

I thought about the gospel song by the Reverend Michael Beckwith and Rickie Byars: "A Deeper Love." It was a love song with God in it.

Then I thought again about the love in the Western world idea that there is one monumental love in a person's life and the rest of the life is spent in yearning. I looked at James Mayo to see if I could see if he was yearning. I thought about the blues tradition, which says that you can move past that lost love and love again with, usually, more cynicism or whimsy or anguish. I tried to understand what he was implying about the gospel tradition. I understood now what he was saying about moving past "being in love to being loving."

While I was thinking, he was saying, "When you love God, then human love is deepened by all the qualities that are in your love of God because you actually experience God in the other person.

"If you look for wrong and deceit in another person, that's what you'll find. If you look for reasons for suspicion and doubt, that's what you'll find.

"But on the other hand, if you are a loving person and you look for contentment, harmony, well-being, beauty, energy, renewal, peace, and love in another person," he said in his hushed voice, "that's what you'll find everywhere you look."

"As long as that person is looking for those same things in you," I said.

"That's what I meant by equally yoked, spiritually. 'Seek and ye shall find,' saith the Bible," he said.

I said, "Okay, now I know what you meant."

"Now suppose you are loving and you're also in love," he suggested.

"Then I would believe that you are over the hurt of Hildah."

"I am," he said. "I really am."

WHAT IF *Love*...?

*W*hat if love could be as Ani wanted it to be, as Ani thought that it must have been a long time ago in Africa, where her parents were born. She was born in New York, but her parents were born in southern Ghana.

"What if love could be like it was back there?" Ani says. "I think it would be better, don't you?"

Her spirit travels back to this place she has never seen. It goes back each morning as she pours libations in her family's apartment. Pouring libations is a ritual that began at a time when Ani's tribe believed that the spirits of ancestors did not depart the earth.

Ani still believes that, to some extent. She does not believe that the spirits of the departed can still act in human affairs, but she believes that humans can get in touch with the spirits as a means of getting in touch with the past, as a means of seeking guidance from the traditions of the past.

She pours libations, a cup of water, for her great-grandmother, her mother's grandmother, Akua, who once lived in the timelessness of the ancient world from which her mother came.

Lately she has been asking Akua for spiritual guidance on love, asking for wisdom from the past on how to understand the mysteries of love in the present.

She pours libations as part of her getting-ready-for-the-day ritual. She performs the ceremony as lovingly as it might have been performed by Akua at the edge of a stream that branched off the

Katawobo, a river in southern Ghana whose name means "cool down your heart."

After Ani's morning ceremony in New York, she wraps her hair in bright orange, red, green, and blue kente cloth using one of the styles that her mother had taught her. Her skirt too is a wrap of the same kente cloth.

"What if a man didn't just marry a woman? What if, instead, he married into her family, married into the traditions of her tribe?" Ani asks as she walks to the subway station at 238th Street and Broadway in the Bronx.

She looks tall, but she is not all that tall. No doubt she seems taller because she is lean, but she isn't skinny. Her limbs are fleshy. She is slender, with long limbs and graceful hands that wave like a bird's wings as she selects a grapefruit and an apple at Kim's fruit-and-vegetable stand near the corner.

I complimented her on our perfect timing. Neither of us was late for the interview that is supposed to take place during most of the day, between classes down at City College, where she is taking a summer course to finish her premedical studies.

The tone of her voice contains a bird's song, especially when she laughs as she pays Kim. She holds a smile as she asks me how am I doing. We make the preliminary conversation and then start our day-long dance of words about love and her broken heart.

"Uhm-m-m," she muses as she pushes onto a number 1 train. It is rush hour, but the train hasn't filled up yet. She is going to speak about the love affair with an African-American guy that just ended. "I think I, I think I just put too much emphasis on me and him. I didn't really take into consideration my family members' feelings about him, because I think when you meet someone it's supposed to be a family process."

We didn't take a seat, but it is not hard for us to talk standing up in the crowd that has filled the train. Most of the people are minding their business. Some may be listening. She doesn't care.

The entire world belongs to us anyway. This is the way I had found her to be back before I decided that I wanted to interview her.

I had thought she would be interesting because she was very much tied to the ancient African view of life as a subjective experience—the external world exists because I experience it, and the only thing that really exists in the external world is what I experience, and the nature of the world is as I experience it in the nowness of this moment.

This view makes the world seem very whole to her, as if everything has been put here for her for some reason that has to do with the working out of her destiny.

"When you're in love you seem to be blind. There's a lot of things that your mate is doing that you either don't see or you can't see. I find that people who claim they love someone, they can't see what the person is doing wrong to them, because they're in love. Things that are so conspicuous to everyone else, you, for some reason, can't see what is so vivid to everyone else."

An older African-American, or maybe West Indian, woman smiles approvingly. She is holding on to the same pole as Ani and me as the number 1 train moves southward, picking up enough passengers to crowd the train even more and make it impossible to stand without people touching you on all sides.

Ani continues: "Meaning that, uhm-m-m-m, usually, for instance, if my brother is interested in a young woman, if he brings her to the house and I don't like her, I don't think he should continue to date her because I think I know my brother and I would know that this girl is not going to be good for him. She isn't the type of person that I can see him with. She might be a girl who isn't going anywhere with herself. She might be a bully. She might be dishonest by nature. She might be too flashy for him, because I know my brother.

"This is true. I see it all the time, but the person in love cannot see it. I can see trouble down the road, but my brother, all he sees is this girl he's supposed to be in love with. The relationships he has had in the past, he didn't see it at first, but after a while he came to see it."

The older woman looks up at me, smiling in a self-satisfied way, as if to say, Amen. Her look says, Listen to this because this is the truth. Ani has drawn her into our world.

Ani continues now, speaking for herself and the woman: "I just think that your family, I think your family, at this point in my life, I can have my family pick a person for me to be with, that's how much faith I have in them. Because I've gone through different people just for my family to be right in the end."

I laugh. The older woman's expression says, Don't laugh. Listen to this. "What about the emotions of it?" I ask. What about love?" I ask in a way that is bound to irritate her.

"To me, uhm, I don't really believe in love the way most people perceive it to be. I think I don't really see the need for love in a relationship. I just think that as long as you respect each other, and you're honest." She laughs because of the mocking expression I put on my face. "Honest." She laughs. "Honest."

"You don't see a need for love that makes the blue skies blue, that makes the birds sing, that makes your heart take wings?" I say in a voice that seems to accuse her of committing sacrilege. "You don't believe in the Icon?"

"What's the Icon?"

I joke. "You don't even know who the Icon is?"

She laughs. "Who?"

"How could anyone not know the Icon?" I scold.

She laughs apologetically.

"Barry White. You don't know that Barry White is the Icon?" I make my voice as deep as I can, trying to duplicate Barry White's booming bass: "Come here, my dear, take off your brassiere."

The little West Indian woman wants to hit me for stringing her out like that. Ani laughs. "No . . . I think that's the problem.

True love is not like you hear it all the time on the radio. The songs on the radio, that's what's got this culture all messed up. That's all they play on the radio, that's all you see on television. I see it as a way to distract people. People get so absorbed in wanting to be with someone. I think it's a distraction. That's what I think."

The West Indian woman is happy now that Ani has gotten things back on track.

"You don't need love to wake you up in the morning? You don't need love to put you to sleep at night?" I say in a how-dare-you-not voice.

"I could marry someone and not love him. I could." Ani laughs in an embarrassed sort of way. "I could be with him, and have children. And the way I see it now, if I think he could be a good father, he's responsible, honest, and trustworthy, and then I think I could marry him."

"Do you think that has something to do with your African cultural background?" I finally get serious again.

"Yes. I remember being young and hearing about arranged marriages, and I thought: 'That's so barbaric.' But now, I could have my mother pick someone for me that I've never met. And I could marry him, because I know she would make a good decision for me. Mostly because I'm not a person that cares too much about physical appearance. You know, what people think is attractive. To me, that just happens to be what the person looks like."

"And you look deeper than that," I say, finally going along with her instead of messing with her.

"Deeper, much deeper," she says. "Much deeper. My mother would look much deeper than physical appearance—whether a man looked good or not."

While she is talking, half my mind begins wondering about her initial statement: what if love today was like that, not that anyone would let it be, but what if?

Back in the ancient days in Africa, Akua's family would have found a young man of another lineage. Over time they would have made inquiries into the family background and character of the prospective husband.

They would have wanted to make sure that Akua married a good man from a good family. This is the way it was done in many folk cultures. It wasn't a marriage for love, as we know love to be. There were, surely in those days, shy and beautiful maidens and brave and handsome young men who sometimes fancied each other, but the family investigation was always performed, because, as Ani said: "The man marries into her family. He marries into the traditions of her tribe." The entire family has to make sure that the fit is right.

"What if love was like that now? It couldn't be, but what if?" she says again, just as if she had plucked the words from my mind at that instant.

The custom was certainly brought to the West Indies and America by African people and, despite slavery, it existed very strongly in an informal way in the islands and the American South until very recently. Who is this young man? Who is this young woman? Where did he or she come from? And the most important of questions: who are his or her people?

The old folks used to ask, "What does his daddy do? Apples don't fall too far from the tree." The old folk didn't have the legal power to stop young people, but the pressure of the community and family could sometimes be as powerful as the law.

The old people used to warn that a suitor is going to be very much like his father. "If you wanta know what kind of woman she'll be, look at her mother," the old people used to say. What if today we put more faith in this ancient wisdom? I think and smile at situations that I know of.

Ani's young man was probably attracted because she was, in the words of older people, comely. Her teeth were perfectly straight and white. Her eyes were bright and clear. He could have fallen in love with her because of her skin. It was as smooth as pitch. He could have fallen in love with her because of her buttocks. She had what the guys called a "nice boot'em-scoot'em."

Or since, in her case, the young man claimed to be Afro-centric, he could have loved the beautiful wraps she wore on her hair, or he could have loved the idea of her.

We often think of the old reasons as being barbaric. What of the new reasons? Often they are just as barbaric. He could have loved her because he wanted to be the center of the world for her.

"Why did you fall in love with him?" I ask as we get off the train at 137th Street.

"Well . . . uhm-m-m-m. He was popular. He was . . . I guess he was African-centered, but . . . that . . . he just talked too much without actually following what he said, basically."

She had to rush to class. She said she would meet me in the lunchroom at eleven-thirty. While she was away at class I sat and thought about what she had said: "Deeper, much deeper . . . than physical appearance—whether a man looked good or not."

I thought about how so much of what is called love in the 1990s is based on physical appearance. I remember a friend who showed me a picture of the woman he had stopped loving and a picture of the one he was now loving. He wanted me to agree that the new one looked better, and that he had bettered his life by getting a better-looking lover.

Love and physical beauty have always been related. Back in Akua's time men and women adorned themselves so that they would look beautiful to each other. The pretty maiden and the handsome young man were valued for their beauty.

Sewa, Ani's mother, Akua's granddaughter, had said earlier that beauty in their language was not simply a matter of the physical features of a person. Sometimes the man or woman with extremely beautiful features "is a spirit in disguise, the spirit of temptation, the spirit of deception, the spirit of arrogance or pride, all disguised as a person." Her laugh was just like that of her daughter.

It was a primitive idea, but you had to think about it. Sewa said that it was impossible for an extremely beautiful person to have strong character. I argued with her for a while because surveys in America seem to prove that better-looking people lead happier lives.

But Sewa was not going to be beaten down on this one. It was part of her observation of life and part of her folk wisdom. She asked me to name one extremely beautiful person who had strong character. When I hesitated, she declared the case closed.

Sewa explained that in her language there is no word for beauty as an abstract concept. Words used to describe beauty have two connotations. "*Tan* means 'ugly,' but it also means 'immoral,' therefore a person can have certain physical characteristics that on another person might look beautiful but on that person they look immoral," she laughed.

I liked Sewa's argument. I didn't necessarily accept it, but I saw it as another valid way of seeing life. *Eso aniwa,* in Sewa's language, means 'it is agreeable to the eye,' but it carries the idea that his or her style of behavior is agreeable to *my* eye, so no matter what one's physical appearance, one could not be *eso aniwa* unless one behaved in a certain way toward me. Toward me—this was the essence of African subjectivity: the world is as I experience it.

No matter what that person's physical features, that person would be *ense*—unacceptable in appearance—if they were not *eso aniwa* to me. It didn't matter how many other people thought this person was *eso aniwa.*

Ahocfew means "graceful" or "elegant," and this is related to the way the person carries his or her body. *Anuounyam* means "nobility of face." "You see, you see," Sewa had said. "It all goes back to character.'' Sewa's manner suggested that she was not to be contradicted. It is law. I wondered for a while: what if it was still the law of how we see each other?

Sewa had a good time explaining how beauty was all tied up with morality, behavior, function, and character. For sensible people it still should be, she said for her daughter's benefit, to keep her daughter from making a mistake by falling in love with someone who simply looked good.

In the old days, Sewa said, a woman could also be judged to be beautiful because she was physically strong for childbearing. "A man can be beautiful because he would make a strong father.''

Sewa was easy to be with, as I had always found Africans to be when you let your spirit flow into acceptance of their culture's view of the world.

The view that I encountered most often with them is that there are a lot of *ense*—unacceptable things about the behavior, functioning, and operation of the world that exists outside the time-honored traditions—but they seem to have a rather robust innocence about their search for things that are *eso aniwa, ahocfew, anuounyam,* especially with regards to love, marriage, and caring for children in extended families.

They seem to hold on to a concept of love that is older than old-fashioned, older than that known by the older woman on the number 1 train, older than the concept of love that our parents in the rural South had tried to keep alive as each generation fell more and more under the sway of the passions excited by African-American love songs created in the blues tradition.

Long before the American experience merged the Western romantic traditions with African rhythms and African spirit–centered ways of being in the world, Akua's family lived a tradition-bound matrilineal life. Akua's mother picked a husband for her and he became a part of her family. Her family lived in a settlement that was headed by Akua's mother's mother and her mother's mother's brother. The extended family was composed of Akua's brothers and sisters and uncles and aunts on the mother's side.

All children born into this family, regardless of whether their parents were married, were cared for by the women. The women worked the farm and the men hunted and fished.

Akua's husband, Oduro, hunted and fished with the men of his extended family, which was headed by his mother's mother and her mother's mother's eldest brother.

Oduro maintained a home for Akua in her settlement and, at times, especially in the evenings, he would bring meat and fish to this home, where he would enjoy the care and the pleasures of Akua, his wife. He would also attend to the male portion of the moral training of his children. This training was also under the care of his children's maternal uncles and older cousins.

As I sat in the lunchroom at City College waiting for Ani, I smiled at the advantages of extended families. I thought about the title President Clinton's wife, Hillary, had used for her book: *It Takes a Village* to raise a child. The title came from a world like Akua's.

In that world disagreements were settled not simply by Akua and her husband but by the entire families of both of them. This was especially effective when the husband's mother favored this "daughter" she had selected for her son and the wife's mother favored this "son" she had selected for her daughter.

This was the way it was in Akua's case. This is the way it was in many cases in the southern United States long ago. Mothers would talk sense into the heads of their own biological children on behalf of sons-in-law or daughters-in-law whom they loved in ways that were much fresher than the ways they loved their own, sometimes troublesome, offspring.

There were also respects paid by each to the other's family. The mother on one side might ask of the mother of the other: "How is my son doing?"

"Oduro is fine. You raised a good boy. I know that Uncle Kwaku likes the *fufu* that Akua fixes. Sorry that we took her away from him. Send one of the children over to fetch some of the fish stew I fixed and some of Akua's *fufu*. Kwaku loves it with a lot of pepper." Debts among family members were not considered debts. No one kept score.

What if this was love in the 1990s? Not the kind that Toni Braxton sings about, the kind that, if you don't get it, you'll "never breathe again." Not the kind that Lisa Lisa & Cult Jam sings about that gets you "lost in emotions," but the kind that is nothing more or less than another part of life.

Even after marriage, both families instructed Akua and her husband about what was right in marriage. Generally, what the husband did in his extended family was none of the wife's business, as long as he respected his wife and brought meat and fish for the children.

The wife was considered to have her own separate life in the overall life of her mother's family. It was a system that accounts for some of the independence of modern women who feel uncomfortable with lives that are subsets of the lives of men in nuclear families.

This is what Ani had wanted in 1994 in New York when she met Raheem, this popular, African-centered, African-American guy who talked so much without actually following what he said.

She came back to the lunchroom after her class ended at eleven-thirty. I ask her: "What did it feel like, being in love?"

She sits down to have for lunch the grapefruit and apple she had bought that morning at Kim's. "It was nice the first month, but after that it was just hell." I can see that she doesn't like to talk about it.

"How long were you going out with this guy?"

"A year."

"And during that time you thought you were in love?"

"Yeah."

"Was he a student at City College?"

"No. But everyone down here knows him. Whenever there is something African-oriented, he's here."

"And you say that it was hell after the first month?"

"Yeah."

"It was very painful?"

"Yeah."

"So, you had a broken heart."

"Yeah."

"What happened?"

"I think he wanted me around him all the time. I think there was too much jealousy. You know, if I had male friends, Raheem might get a little bothered and that might lead to other problems. Possessiveness. He had time and I didn't, and if you don't have time for him, he took it personal."

"He was afraid he couldn't trust you?"

"I think he trusted me. I think he was the person that couldn't be trusted, so he pushed that onto me and thought that was a problem for both of us, so therefore we should be together all the time."

"You mean he couldn't trust himself?"

"Yes, that was it."

"Because he was messing?"

"No, but he was attracted to other people. And he thought that of me."

"You were not attracted to anybody."

"No. But I might think a person is attractive, but that doesn't mean I'll be attracted to them. I have to get to know a person for a long time. Screen him."

"Did you screen Raheem?"

"I thought I had. He used to come to a lot of Afro-centric things here at City College. I watched him and he seemed so sincere. We talked and it wasn't like he was trying to talk *to* me, which is the way I like it.

"That's the way I thought I was being, screening him, but I got blinded. I thought he thought I was interacting with him on a formal, businesslike basis in various activities. But actually I was looking for some qualities. I thought I was carefully screening him.

"I didn't let him know that I liked him. Normally I would be looking for someone on my same intellectual level, someone you can talk to on the same level, have an intellectual conversation with. I wanted someone who cared for me a lot. He seemed that he did. I thought that I could probably grow to care for him.

"I normally want someone who is responsible. I hate laziness— someone who needs to be pushed. Someone you have to coax to do something with their life. And then there were the usual things—honesty, trust, you know.

"I'm also a spiritual person too."

"What do you mean?"

"I believe in the ancestors. I wanted someone who believed in that. I believe they are with us. Believe there's more to life than just this." She spread her hands out and looked around to indicate the material world.

"I believe in meditating. And I never thought I would find a man who believed in these things. All I was hoping for was a man who could respect the fact that I believe in them, but then I was screening Raheem and he said he believed in all of this.

"He meditated. He fasted. He prayed to the ancestors—the whole thing. That's why I say that love is blind. My mother knew that these things were just talk, but I didn't know because I was blinded. Gradually I had fallen in love with Raheem, but still he didn't know.''

"Did you want to marry him?" I ask.

"Yeah. My mother said that sometimes when you find an African American who believes in these things, that's all that they do. They don't want a job. They just want to be Afro-centric, read a few books and burn some incense. I couldn't see that.

"Then I noticed that when I didn't give him all my attention, he would get disrespectful."

"How?"

"Well, to me he was flirty-flirty, to the extent where it was disrespectful, you know what I mean? But I took it as, well, he was flirty, and I'm not a jealous person, but then he told me he wanted to date other people, and he began talking about polygamy. He kept saying that the African man was naturally polygamous.''

"Did he want to get married to you?"

"Initially. But later on no. But he's gonna be married soon. He has a baby on the way.''

"Hummmm," I laugh.

"Hummmm," she laughs.

"He really hurt you bad, huh?"

"Yeah.''

"So you did have your heart into it."

"Yeah.''

"So you really do believe in love."

"No, I don't. Not at all." She flies into a mock rage. "About a month after he and I started going together, my life went into a decline, like my life was going down, and now it's kinda coming back up.

"My mother was right. Anything she says I just do right now, because it's really for the best because my life has dramatically improved since I stopped seeing Raheem. The stress of a relationship can really wear someone down. There are just things that I don't have to worry about or deal with anymore, worry about how come he didn't call me today. You know, sometimes we may have had an argument and then you can't concentrate for the rest of the day. You know, just things like that. Now I just pray and meditate.''

"For someone to love?'' I ask, and sing a little bit of the happy song by Sam Cooke, which was also a prayer that God send someone to love.

"I don't pray for that. You don't pray and meditate to get God to give you something, or to make your life better. You pray and meditate to find peace so you can have the strength to make it better. You pray and meditate to find a sense of spiritual completeness so that from a sense of wholeness we are divinely guided to be and do what is necessary to get done what we were put on earth to do.

"That was part of the problem. Raheem wanted to pray and have a blessing fall out of the sky to him,'' she laughs. "Another problem, he would always talk about you should be with a strong woman, and you should learn from each other. But there were certain things that would come up that I happened to know about more than him. He disliked that a lot. He couldn't deal with it. He just has to be in the spotlight, the center of attention. He likes to know everything.

"Well, I'm happy he has a baby on the way, and everything; and I hope that whoever is his current girlfriend, that they're happy together.''

"And you're happy being by yourself?''

"Very much so!''

"What's so happy about being by yourself? Don't you feel a need for somebody?''

"No. I don't. Because that's the thing. I always . . . up until this point I always felt lonely, now I'm just alone.''

"What about a physical, sexual need?"

"No. No, I don't."

"Why do you think you don't?"

"I don't know. Honestly, I don't know."

"Well, if you don't feel it, you don't need to worry about it."

"The act is important, but for me it's just . . . I don't know, sex is just a physical manifestation of the relationship. When the relationship isn't going good, the act is just irritating to me. It's really no big deal to me."

"I can hear all the black male egos from all around the country saying, 'She just hasn't met me yet. If she meets me I would make love to her all night long. When she got one dose of this thing, she would be "Dancing in the Street." I would "Ride Your Pony." ' "

Because I know she is annoyed by the way love is depicted in American popular music, I use the names of songs to tease her about all the things that a man who would consider himself a "Good Rocking Daddy" would say to a woman who said that "Jelly Rolling" was no big deal.

I sing: " 'Try me,' as James Brown would say. 'You better know it,' as Jackie Wilson would say. 'Call on me,' as Bobby 'Blue' Bland would say."

"Please!" she says, laughing.

"That's the song. James Brown, 'Please, Please, Please.' "

She continues laughing.

"The boys would say: 'I'd make her climax all over herself. Sh-i-i-i-t, it's just because she hasn't been fucked right. That's all.' "

She laughed. "When the relationship is going well, then the act is beautiful, right?"

"I guess."

"I don't know."

"That's what they say."

"I don't think I've found the person and you know, I just . . . It's never been that great for me, never. So it's not like I'm missing much. As opposed to people who had this great experience."

"Maybe you haven't found the right person. Because you do believe in what some people say: that the act is fantastic."

"I do believe it. I have friends that say that it is. I guess I haven't met the right person. Society makes people want to fall in love. Because if you think about it, that's all basically all the songs that they play on the radio are about—love or someone's heart is broken or someone is falling in love, you know, some relationship in some form."

"What do you prefer to love?"

"Oh, responsibility."

"Responsible for what?"

"For your life. What your life careers are. What your life's goals are gonna be. Things like that." She starts to laugh again.

"A good meal, a walk in the woods. All that stuff can be better, huh?" I finally decide to let her know that I know what she means, and that I am capable of wondering if love was not as it was depicted in the songs. What if it was deeper, much deeper, embedded in the life of community?

"You say you've heard this song by Toni Braxton, 'Breathe Again'?" she asks.

"Yeah."

She recites a portion of it as if she knows it because she has thought about it often. The song says that if this woman doesn't get this man back into her arms, she will never breathe again.

I pull all the way in on her side. "Isn't that silly," I tease.

"People get like that," she says.

"I know," I say.

"I was like that," she says.

I added fuel to the fire she was building for our amusement: " 'How Am I Supposed to Live Without You.' "

" 'I Want to Be Your Everything,' " she says with mock contempt.

" 'Everything I Do, I Do For You,' " I say with amused disdain.

"I used to hear all these songs when I was making up my mind about Raheem. So I can't really say that I was in love. Throughout my life, I'm always hearing about love. I think I was in love with love and I just started loving the person who happened to be there. That's what happened, 'cause every time we turn around there's a love story on television or you're reading about it, or you're hearing about it or someone's telling you about it. I think I just became in love with it, and not really him per se, he just happened to be a nice person."

"Or he pretended to be," I say. "What did you offer him? Maybe he was flirty because he didn't think you loved him enough. Maybe his ego needed you to give him more attention. Maybe he wanted to be your everything and when he couldn't be he wanted to date other women."

"I'm not perfect," she says. "But he always said he loved me because I have a unique personality. I think I'm unique, because a lot of things I do are intriguing."

"Like what?"

"My manner. My way. My mystery as a woman. He always likes to talk to me. He always said he's never met anyone like me. I make people see the positive light in a situation."

"To a man those things might feel more like friendship than love, as we know it. What about the emotional things, the romantic part. You're physically a very beautiful woman. He would want you to show you were head over heels in love so he could feel adequate in love."

"I don't know. I don't think I'm good at the emotional thing.

I'm very good with talking and making a man feel good and helping him, but the contact part, no, I'm not good at that. I confess. I'm the kind of person that get's annoyed when I see people who do any open display. I find that insulting. Holding hands is okay. But I don't do more than that. Anything that goes beyond a light kiss.''

''But you and your family hug all the time.''

''I know, that's my family.''

''You know what the secret is?''

''What?''

''The secret is in your name.'' I decide to have some more fun with Ani. ''Your full name, Animoyam?''

She smiled. ''Animoyam Youaa Enka Yarme,'' she says. She slows it down so I can get it, and then she lets it roll off her tongue quickly, as she would pronounce it to someone from her country.

''It means 'All Praises to God,' right?''

''Yes.''

''Well, in the Western world men want some of those praises to come to them. Black men especially, after he's just spent his money to wine you and dine you and he's just made what he considers the best love that anyone has ever made to anyone since the beginning of time, he wants your name to be 'All Praises to Raheem,' '' I say, and flex my muscles as Raheem would.

She starts laughing. She can't stop laughing.